T0115268

Advance Praise for *Your Faith Has Made You Well*

"Well done! The most fundamental theological argument is healing and wholeness is not something that is magically/miraculously provided by God's hand without our involvement, but that it is what can happen when we involve ourselves with God—through prayer, through our pursuit of faith, through connecting our stories to the biblical stories.... I resonate deeply with this conviction."

— Gil Rendle, Author and Ordained Minister with the United Methodist Church

"I'm especially grateful for Bruce's approach for those of us who are always searching for accessible and honest resources and practical guidance in growing our faith. Bruce uses a wonderful variety of contemporary and biblical stories to help us understand how God can work in extraordinary ways through ordinary people who are also willing to work with God."

— Tom Locke, President of the Texas Methodist Foundation

"For the first time in my life, I read a book from start to finish in a single seating. I found this book easy to read and impossible to put down. A compliment! I can easily relate to the characters and the wonderful stories told throughout the book."

— Emmitt Gibson, Retired 2-star General, Army

"The chapters on Prayer and Grieving were the ones that resonated with me the most. I was glad to see just how personal our prayers can be and how much God wants us to communicate with Him. I pray that people reading the book will be encouraged to try the ways the book suggested, in order to lead them to a more intimate prayer life. The book will be therapeutic to readers!"

— Nancy Duttry, Advance Reader

"A solid and extraordinarily well written book. Theologically the book is well constructed and accurate. I appreciated the stories and connection to the Gospels. A Jesus-centric book that reminds us of that Christ is the central and guiding force in our lives. Hope precedes faith, which in turn precedes trust in God. This book elegantly ties this concept together."
— Ken Mann, Senior Pastor, Baptist Church

"Dr. Hartman is a wise man with a warm heart."
— Dr. Heather Murray Elkins, Author of *Holy Stuff of Life*

Also by Dr. Bruce L. Hartman

*Jesus & Co.: Connecting the Lessons of The Gospel
with Today's Business World*

YOUR FAITH HAS MADE YOU WELL

A Radical New Way to Create Peace and Hope

DR. BRUCE L. HARTMAN

A POST HILL PRESS BOOK
ISBN: 978-1-64293-213-3
ISBN (eBook): 978-1-64293-214-0

Your Faith Has Made You Well:
A Radical New Way to Create Peace and Hope
© 2019 by Dr. Bruce L. Hartman
All Rights Reserved

Cover art by Tricia Principe
principedesign.com

Post Hill Press
New York • Nashville
posthillpress.com

Published in the United States of America

TABLE OF CONTENTS

PROLOGUE

"Take heart, daughter; your faith has made you well."
—MATTHEW 9:22

Standing Alone in Front of God

In the first century, standing on the side of a road, pressed in by a throng of onlookers, a woman stood waiting for Jesus to pass by. Waiting for what seemed like her final chance to be healed. For twelve long years she had been hemorrhaging from a disease that had isolated her from her community and forced her to live on the outskirts of society. For twelve years she had spent what little money she had on doctors, only to have her health continue to decline. Frightened and scarred by the isolation caused by her disease, she desperately wanted to be healed. Faithfully, she stood there waiting for "The One" to pass by so she could touch his cloak and be healed.

Apparent in this story is the specific nature of the social isolation that occurred with the woman's persistent bleeding. By the standards of the first century, she was considered "unclean." As such, she was banned from communal activities and, like the lepers of her time, forced to live away. Like most people, she could adjust to her situation, but just beneath the surface of her forced acceptance, she desired human contact and affirmation of her existence. Loneliness was a constant companion.

There he was, close enough to touch. As he passed by, she forced her way through the enormous crowd, came up behind him, and lay her fingers upon his cloak. Instantly, she felt that her disease had been cured. He turned around and looked for the person who had touched him. The crowd was thick and pressed in around him; his disciples were confused that he asked who had touched him. The woman emerged from the crowd and said that it was she. There, trembling in fear, she stood face-to-face with "The One." Despite the multitude, she now stood alone, looking into the eyes of God.

Jesus, looking into the eyes of a desperate person, saw the pureness of her faith. In that moment, he affirmed her existence as one of God's children and said to her, *"Take heart, daughter; your faith has made you well."* For twelve years she had tried everything possible to escape from her despair. In an instant, with incredible courage and faith, she had stepped through the crowd and found her answer: Jesus. The many long nights of searching for a solution were now at an end. She was whole again. A simple, brave act of reaching out to touch the cloak of God had changed the course of her life. Jesus had affirmed her existence and faith. She now belonged and was healed!

How many times in our lives have we searched for an answer, running down all the corridors of our mind in search of a solution, trying everything only to find nothing works? We become despondent, knowing that despite all our earnest efforts we have not moved forward. Then, when we finally relent, give in to our faith, and pray, we find our answer. The simple act of prayer combined with our own efforts produces a solution of hope. A simple act of faith heals us. A simple act that becomes a very personal experience with God. An act of faith that not only heals us but also lets us know God is with us and loves us.

✝ ✝ ✝

Using Prayer and Faith to Create a Miracle

I was sitting in a restaurant with friends when Ed approached, wearing a solemn look. I could tell by his demeanor that he had bad news—his normal smile was gone. Ed relayed to me that "Scott is in trouble." Scott's wife, Cindy, had called Ed and asked him to let a few of us know that we needed to pray hard for Scott. His life was in peril.

A few days earlier, Scott had gone in for a minor surgical procedure. In the process, doctors had made a grievous error causing a septic infection. Scott was now being prepped for a second surgery to resolve this unanticipated and extremely serious medical issue. Barely alert, he had asked the doctor, "Am I going to be all right?" The surgeon replied, "I can't make any promises."

At the same time, Cindy sent out that call for prayer through Ed. Individually and as a group we began our prayers. Prayers for healing and recovery. Scott survived the surgery but remained gravely ill. We formed a prayer chain and sent these prayers to Cindy daily by text. These prayers were developed from very deep meditation, and each contained a heartfelt plea to save our friend. In the texts we called on Jesus to intercede, and each intercessional prayer included the statement, *"We pray in Jesus's name."*

Over the next few days, things remained very touch and go. I could tell by Cindy's responses that there were moments of both hope and despair. Desperately, she continued urging us to pray. Each day, I went into the deepest part of my being, searching for a message that I could send to her. In these moments, I became extraordinarily focused in asking God for help. After a week of these mornings of quiet solitude in a very deep state of prayer, and sensing her worry but also her deep faith, I sent her the scripture about the bleeding woman and her miraculous recovery. I also told her that, through my prayers, I had come to feel a deep sense of conviction that her faith would make Scott well.

Cindy is a quiet woman with extraordinary common sense. Any question I'd ever asked her was always answered directly and clearly. Her replies were as elegant as they were simple. I also knew her to have the same approach with her faith. She is a deeply faithful woman who relies on God during the turbulent times in her life. Moreover, she is also thankful to God for the many blessings in her life. Her faith is undeniably evident and unvarnished. She believes from her heart.

Because I knew her great faith, I knew that, in this dark time, she would be able to identify with the woman who touched Jesus's cloak. She spent the balance of the day thinking about that woman and continually forced her own faith to connect with the unseen. She continued to push away the darkness and, in her mind, stayed riveted on Jesus, mirroring the same faith as the bleeding woman from Matthew 9:22.

Scott did recover, slowly, over a long period of recovery that stretched from days to weeks and then to two months. Not long after, I remember visiting my friend with little to say; I just wanted to bask in his presence and spiritually feel his recovery. I sat there just looking at his eyes, which were bright again. He said, "God saved me. I am a lucky man." Silently, I knew both his and Cindy's faith had healed him.

✟ ✟ ✟

Each Person's Faith Journey Is Unique and Personal

These two stories are wonderful examples of the value of faith and its miraculous effect on human lives. These simple moments resulted in miracles born from a history of developing a faith-life and a commitment to God. In these kinds of history, which many of us share, are moments of despair, questioning, and resilience. Moments when the world tries to pull us away, and moments when we get undeniable truth.

This book is about faith; it's not a prescriptive how-to book, but a collection of stories designed to create a sense of wonder and imagination about faith. No one arrives at faith through someone else's lens but through their own history and personal relationship with Jesus. Each journey is unique and personal; perhaps it is like others in some ways, but in its intimacy, it is special to the individual. For some, finding faith is like hitting the button in an elevator. They push the button for the top floor, and they arrive. But for most, it is a journey of discovery. A journey that can be aided by others but that is ultimately defined by individual experiences and the inevitable gazing into the eyes of God. A personal journey, with life's valleys and peaks.

✝ ✝ ✝

We Yearn to Know Jesus

Early in the Gospel of John, Jesus was walking on a road followed by two men. Sensing their presence, he turned and asked, *"What are you looking for?"* (John 1:38) Their answer was what we all are looking for. To be with Jesus and have Jesus in our hearts. Those walking with Jesus on the road in ancient Judea also wanted to know Jesus. They wanted to have the presence of Christ in their hearts. They wanted a deeper relationship than just knowing Christ existed. Like many of us, they wanted their hearts to be connected to God through His son.

Matthew Henry, the famed theological scholar from the seventeenth century, called this kind of changed experience that of *"an awakened soul."* It is a communion between our souls and Christ. Christ begins the conversation by asking, **"What are you looking for?"** When we hear this question deep within our hearts and souls, the process of fully accepting Jesus has begun. By answering Christ's question, we begin the journey to a singular focus on our faith.

A faith that Jesus exists, is with us, and is what we are looking for. A faith in the unseen that heals us from the troubles of our world. A faith that becomes our refuge when we are left disrupted.

✞   ✞   ✞

Our Faith Will Make Us Well

Our faith will make us well. Perhaps it will be through divine intervention. More likely, it occurs from our own investment in concert with God. There are times when we have invested all we have to give and see few results; then God intercedes, and our efforts pay off. For every act of real healing, there is a combination of our efforts and God's intervention. There is no formula for how much we must invest; sometimes it's a little and sometimes a lot. Each healing lies somewhere on this continuum of faith.

For the bleeding woman, it was an extraordinary personal investment. She knew through faith that Jesus could help her. Hers was a faith so strong that she defied the social standards of the first century and forced herself through a mighty throng to touch Jesus's cloak. For Cindy, it was a knowledge that her prayers and those of her neighbor would save Scott. For Scott himself, it was the fortitude to hang tough and believe. They didn't wait around for God—they acted.

Eight times in the Gospels Jesus says, in some form, *"Your faith has made you well."* This book is about developing this healing faith and how others have achieved it.

✟   ✟   ✟

Bringing Our Faith to the Surface

A healing faith comes from a life of following Jesus. Not just praying to be healed but from developing a connection and relationship with Jesus. The faith that heals us comes from a concerted desire to be connected to Jesus. This journey often requires many valleys and peaks. It is a journey that must continuously be explored. Like all adventures, it has many chapters. Through our struggles, our faith matures. If our faith has not been tested, we are long overdue.

This book contains the stories of almost fifty people. Many I interviewed and some were researched. I discovered that most faith stories exist just below the surface of our projected state of normalcy. Deep stories from a life of yearning to know God. Stories of success and disappointment with their faith and lives. In my interviews, the discussions became very personal, and I observed that these discussions of faith-lives brought extraordinary emotion to the surface. Sometimes there were tears not from sorrow, but from the raw emotion of their lives and faith. Gil Rendle, the wonderful author of many Christian books, said to me: *"I see this yearning in America. A desire to know and grow strong in their faith. A constant under-the-surface desire to be connected to a compelling and loving God."* Gil is right; I saw the same thing during my interviews.

All of the people in this book are real. In some cases, the names have been changed to protect privacy. In others, the facts are somewhat obscured, also to protect privacy. These people gave all they had for others to see, and hopefully benefit from, their journeys. The people in this book represent many varieties and seasons of faith that show the many unique roads that may be taken. All reflect a faith that heals.

The book contains two parts. Part One, called "The Fundamentals of Faith," is an explanation of our faith. It details how others have achieved faith through a connected life with Jesus and the value of prayer. In this section is also a theological explanation of who Jesus is as seen through the Bible.

Part Two is called "The Seasons of Faith." We all acquire our faith differently. For some it begins as a blind faith that evolves into understanding, where they say, *"I was blind, but now I see."* For others it comes when there is no other place to turn, as it did for C. S. Lewis, who fought for years before succumbing to the inevitable and compelling force of God. Others find their faith through a giving nature that cements their life's purpose as being made in the image of God. For many, there are times when we experience the many seasons of faith separately during our lifetime.

There are stories in this book when prayers were answered and also when they were not. When they were not, where did the storytellers turn? Did they bear into God or turn away? Each road is different, but each is relatable as each of us move through the seasons of our own faith.

Each journey will lead us to *"rejoice in hope, be patient in suffering, and persevere in prayer."* (Romans 12:12)

Have faith!

Part One

~

The Fundamentals of Faith

Developing a faith that makes us well, involves knowing the fundamentals of faith. Specifically, three things: *What is faith? How does prayer help? And who is Jesus?* Chapters one through three explore these fundamentals.

The first chapter is about defining faith and expanding how we think about faith. Chapter Two explores prayer as a gateway to developing faith. It is a more technical chapter that includes examples of how to pray. Chapter Three is about Jesus, specifically asking the question: *"What sort of man is he?"* This chapter expands on who Jesus is, lifting him up from being a single thought to many thoughts. In addition, the chapter goes into a very specific view of Jesus as seen through the words of the Bible, that Jesus is both with God and *is* God. Part One lays the foundation for Part Two, which addresses *"The Seasons of Faith"* in our lives.

CHAPTER 1
FAITH AND THE MUSTARD SEED

*"For truly I tell you, if you have faith the size of a mustard
seed, you will say to this mountain, 'Move from here to there,'
and it will move; nothing will be impossible for you."*

—MATTHEW 17:20

Turning Our Lives Over to God

On October 31, 2003, Bethany Hamilton was surfing
along Tunnels Beach in Hawaii. As this young surfing phenom
lay on her surfboard waiting for the swell that would allow her
to carve a familiar line in the breaking wave, a tiger shark swam
up from underneath her and seized hold of her dangling left
arm. The razor-sharp teeth of the shark severed her left arm and
left Bethany dazed and bleeding profusely in the water. She was
adrift, terrified, and losing her grip on life.

People from the beach and other surfers hurried to help get
her back to shore. Once on the beach, the father of one of the
surfers hurriedly applied a tourniquet to stop the bleeding. A
doctor who lived nearby had heard about the attack and fran-
tically rushed to her aid. He stayed at her side and attended
to her on the way to the hospital. She'd lost 60 percent of her

blood volume. Coincidently, her father was scheduled to have knee surgery that same morning. Upon learning about the grave situation, he immediately gave up his slot, and Bethany was successfully operated on. She was only thirteen.

While she was in recovery, she and her mother prayed. They prayed that God would use this accident for his glory. After a week, Bethany was released, and she began to think about the national surfing championships that were scheduled in two months—an unimaginable thought for someone who had just barely survived a shark attack that left her with only one arm. She continued to pray and focus on her faith. She recovered with remarkable speed. Not only did she participate in the championships—she won. All with one arm and being only two months removed from her accident. She had come close to dying, and a remarkable set of events had saved her life. Winning the title with one arm was even more remarkable; in fact, it seemed impossible.

When things seem impossible, Jesus asks us to believe and have faith. In Matthew 17:20, Jesus says, ***"For truly I tell you, if you have faith the size of a mustard seed, you will say to this mountain, 'Move from here to there,' and it will move; nothing will be impossible for you."*** This is the spot Jesus wants us to move to—a place of believing in all possibilities. There may be times when it doesn't appear that unlimited possibilities exist, but there are far many more times when we will see God at work in our lives. Through both the low points and successes of our lives, our faith can be strengthened. We are able to experience richer faith-lives through the observations of God's involvement in our lives.

> *"Jesus points out that we, as mortals, can view things as impossible, but to God all is possible."*

Jesus points out that we, as mortals, can view things as impossible, but to God all is possible. When we pray, we have a chance. When we pray with all our heart, we can succeed. Bethany and her mom asked God to help—not for their glory, but for God's. Theirs was a heart of faith designed to show that despite overwhelming odds, God could do the impossible.

We have all had those times when it seemed like doom awaited us. We worry, and we pace. We wonder, *what is the answer?* How do we overcome? We overcome when we change our focus from us to God. When we turn our eyes to God and leave behind our thoughts of despair, we give God space to work in our lives. It may not be as remarkable as it was with Bethany Hamilton but, for us personally, it will still be dramatic. God's answer will be unique and very intimate. Through God's answer, because of its uniqueness and intimacy, we will know we belong to God. Our faith becomes strengthened.

✟   ✟   ✟

Faith Is a Belief in the Unseen

The biggest impediment to our faith is ourselves. Not because we are weak, unworthy, or inherently bad, but because we trust too much in what we see, what we have learned, and what we think. Faith is a belief in the unseen. Our human instincts and our own senses can often drive us away from faith. If we cannot see, we think we cannot believe. From the day we are born, our senses teach us what to trust and believe. Our very survival depends on this trust, but at the same time those senses push us away from believing in the unseen. As we age, we learn to trust only in what we know, touch, feel, see, and surmise, creating a barrier that becomes harder each day for our faith to burst through.

> *"Our hearts are unquiet until they rest in God."*

Saint Augustine, one of the church's early leaders, said, *"Our hearts are unquiet until they rest in God."* A powerful statement from a man who, until his mid-thirties, engaged in a life very far away from God. He was originally a great lawyer and orator. His fame was so widespread that he was recruited to go to Rome to teach aspiring students about oratory, reading, and philosophy. Augustine was one of the few in the fourth century who could read and write at a very high level. During this period of his life he was in constant pursuit of the *"truth."* He relied on finding this *"truth"* through earthly means and his own intellect. If he could not use reason to understand what was real, then it was not real. Yet despite his great ability to reason, he kept slipping further away from finding the *"truth."*

His mother, Monica, a deeply faithful woman, spent a good deal of her life pushing her son to look to God for the *"truth."* At each turn Augustine rebuffed her attempts, considering her efforts superstitious. Finally, after many failed attempts at finding the *"truth,"* and encouraged by his mother, he met with Bishop Ambrose in Milan. Through many meetings with the bishop, Augustine discovered that he had been on the wrong path to real truth. Bishop Ambrose showed Augustine that the *"truth"* resided in the unseen.

In a garden in Milan, sitting alone with his thoughts and in despair over his life's journey, he heard a child's voice. He became convinced this was the voice of Jesus, and in this moment, he knelt to accept Jesus as the *"truth."* Augustine went on to become a bishop himself and was ultimately the key figure in firmly propelling the Christian church during the fourth century. After a lifetime of *thinking* about the truth, he discovered that it had never been far away; *"truth"* resided in his heart. A place that does not rationalize but believes. A place where both our joy and our pain reside. It is here our hearts are quieted and where we have faith in the unseen.

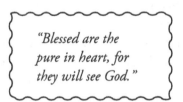

"Blessed are the pure in heart, for they will see God."

One of Jesus's first acts was to deliver a powerful sermon revealing his mission on earth. It is known as the Sermon on the Mount. In it Jesus says, ***"Blessed are the pure in heart, for they will see God."*** (Matthew 5:8) Jesus tells us in this verse to have a pure heart. A heart led to do good. One that avoids the temptation to give in to our fears, desires, and schemes. A heart that reaches out to our neighbor. A heart that has faith in God. A heart that endures momentary losses and looks to the future. A heart of hope in the unseen. Jesus asks us to not give in to our personal power but to our hearts and the intrinsic human desire to do good as images of God. It is here we will see God and find our faith.

Augustine found his faith in his heart. He found it by looking not for the seen but for the unseen. After a lifetime of disquiet, for the remainder of his life his heart became quieted.

✛ ✛ ✛

The Spiritual Value of a Faithful and God-Centered Heart

A friend of mine named Donna talks about this state of a having a "quieted heart" and trusting in the unseen as it relates to her own life and her dream of owning a business. After a difficult period early in her life that involved alcoholism and challenging times with her parents, Donna found Jesus. She recovered from her addiction and became a new creation through Christ. Over the next few years, she began to pray regularly and searched for a new direction. During these prayers, she found the strength and faith to embrace a life-long dream of being an independent businessperson. Through deep personal sacrifice, she saved up enough money to start a business. She bought a building and broke it up into smaller offices to create an office-share business. Despite competition from bigger companies, she built a successful business that today includes numerous other buildings and many customers. She let go of her fears and the alcohol that soothed her fears. She began to thrive. She learned the importance of faith and, when coupled with her own efforts, was healed and became a successful businessperson.

At the various crossroads of this amazing story of revival, Donna focused on two things. The first was to make ethical decisions; the second, was to listen for God's direction with a "quieted heart." Donna's personal investment in her life through being virtuous and maintaining a rock-steady faith helped both her business and her relationship with God. She tells me that over time, at each of her business crossroads, it was her faith that guided her decisions and led her to success.

Jesus asks us to have a faithful heart and follow its direction. There are times when our hearts appear wrong or we are beset with worry. But if our hearts are God-centered and faithful, we will survive and most likely thrive. Decisions that are made with the wrong intentions, however, will nag us in the future. Sleeping and our overall sense of well-being improve when we act with a pure heart. The momentary losses that sometimes stand temporarily in our way will disappear over time. Through faith our hearts will become quiet and at rest. Our *"quieted hearts"* heal us spiritually and provide a firm bedrock for daily life.

☩   ☩   ☩

Taking the "Narrow Gate"

Our faith is something that must be nurtured and sought after. The world reaches out to us and pulls us away through life's temptations, setbacks, and imagined responsibilities. At times the world will convince us that God is not with us, that God is just some imaginary human construct. We will begin to blame others for our problems and to seek easier paths. However, it is at exactly this spot that we should turn from our human instincts and dig deeper into our faith.

The recognition of the sovereign nature of God ebbs when we pay too much attention to the ways of the world and give in to despair. When we turn our eyes to God, the ways of the world grow dimmer, and our faith becomes brighter. A strong faith is practiced and nurtured. There are few roads that are easy with faith. Jesus explains this, with a call to stay steady with our faith, when he says, ***"For the gate is narrow and the road is hard that leads to life and there are few who find it."*** (Matthew 7:14)

In life, it is often the little things that make a difference. Our faith-lives are similar. For instance, great musicians do not move on from practice until all notes are played correctly. Great painters ignore the clock until every blemish is resolved. Many of us face these types of decisions in our work lives as well. Do we stop to get things right or allow limited time to force us to sacrifice quality in order to check off a "to do"? Inevitably, creating great music, art, or faith takes longer than we expect, and there are always a few more things to do than we anticipated. But it is in this spot with our faith that we must decide between quality and quantity. Do we finish our task because time is telling us to move on, or do we dig deeper to resolve those nagging feelings? This spot reminds me of a quote I used many times in my career: *"The great enemy of art is time."* Likewise, our faith-life can become victim to the suffocating drumbeat of time. High-quality faith requires a focus to go deeper in practicing our faith. How often do we say, *"I cannot do any more"* or *"I do not have the time to nurture my faith"* and move on? It is this internal decision that separates great faith from faith that is just an afterthought.

Our faith is in investment in ourselves, in concert with God. God is not a genie that solves our problems alone. Our God is a loving God who desires a relationship with us. Like any relationship, it requires mutual acts of support. There are times when we need more from God than we can give, and God responds. Other times, God only needs to stand by and watch us succeed. This continuum of faith varies from moment to moment.

Many of us are pressed for time. Our to-do list piles up if we tarry too long on a project. We are besieged by an endless list of tasks. Jesus suggests we avoid becoming slaves to our to-do lists and to focus instead on what counts, to be concerned about quality. Jesus wants us to trade off the trivial for the important, to avoid distractions and not stop until we find the answer that settles our souls. Jesus wants us to travel life's narrow gate and take the long road. When we do, many times we find our answer around a corner that looks steep and hard. Faith requires a little more patience, with the sure knowledge that it will still all come together. When we take the time to find the *right* answer, life becomes revealed, and we find peace. We no longer feel defeated or harried. We have climbed a long hill. We have put aside the great enemy of faith: time.

✝ ✝ ✝

Valleys of Despair Are Times of Preparation

In our faith-lives, we sometimes enter valleys of despair. It is our time in these valleys of despair that we should see as periods of preparation. Preparation for the next climb with our faith and God's purpose for us.

After his dramatic conversion on the road to Damascus, the apostle Paul was forced to spend three years in the Arabian desert. Lonely years of preparation. Utterly alone and wondering if his faith in Jesus was worth the cost. He wanted to help spread the message of the "good news" quickly but found himself instead alone in Arabia. But God was readying Paul for a longer journey outside of his known world—the larger mission of spreading Christianity beyond the confines of Judea. During these three desolate years in the desert, God was preparing Paul for three remarkable journeys that would propel Christianity to become the predominate faith of the known world. In the history of Christianity, few missions were as critical as Paul's in spreading the "good news" about Jesus.

> "The key to success isn't what you learn in success, but what you learn in failure."

Peter Drucker, the famed business advisor, says, "The key to success isn't what you learn in success, but what you learn in failure." Consider the following: Winston Churchill was banished from his political party for a decade before he became prime minister. He then led England at a time when they stood alone against the forces of tyranny during World War II. Thomas Edison's teachers told him he was not smart enough. Oprah Winfrey was fired from her first television job as an anchor. Walt Disney was fired by a newspaper because he lacked imagination! We all know the happy endings these stories have. The key ingredient was not giving up but instead getting prepared!

In our own efforts of faith, we should see valleys as a time of preparation. These periods can be an indication of powerful movements that lay ahead in our lives—new directions that God is going to take us in.

Most of us want success, peace, health, and a strong connection with God. Having these dreams and ambitions is critical to moving forward. Wanting to be a virtuous and faithful person or to be good at our craft is a great start. *With our spiritual life, success requires endurance and patience.* When Jesus says to go through the narrow gate, he is telling us to avoid the easy way. He is telling us to respect what we seek. He is telling us that what we seek is sacred. He's asking, *"**Are you willing to put in the time to develop our faith?**"*

✞   ✞   ✞

Embracing the Light of Faith

Chris Gardner, the real-life main character in the movie *The Pursuit of Happyness*, was at various times homeless, a foster child, a single dad, and penniless. He rose to be one of the first African Americans to start a brokerage firm. When asked, *"Where did you discover your faith?"* he replied, *"My mom. I chose to embrace the faith and light I saw in my mom."* He went on to say he could have embraced darkness and given in to a hard early life but chose instead to pursue the light of Jesus that he saw in his mother.

Life was not easy for Chris. An abusive stepfather forced him at times to live in a foster home. He enlisted in the Navy and then went on to start a business selling medical devices. However, his business failed, and his wife left both him and his two-year-old son. Chris then entered an internship program with Dean Witter, a brokerage firm. Unpaid for six months and with only a 5 percent chance of getting hired, he sold all he owned to survive in the program. Along the way, he and his son were evicted from their apartment, thrown out of a motel room, and spent weeks sleeping in a subway station, but Chris never gave up on his dreams. He followed his Plan A, which meant embracing the light of faith his mother had shown him.

Outwardly, Chris expressed a positive and trustworthy attitude that allowed him to gain clients for his firm. He was unfailingly optimistic and faithful and, as you would guess, he became the stockbroker he wanted to be. Seven years later he started his own firm. After twenty-five years of running a successful business, he sold it and has since become a philanthropist and an inspirational speaker.

In the last Gospel, John, there is an abundance of the word "light"—more than in any of the other three Gospels. The unusual number of references encourages us to consider the meaning of light. Light encompasses many things that are good, but most importantly, it is the light of Jesus, the Way, and an alternative to despair and broken dreams. The Book of John uses the imagery of light as a contrast to darkness, which represents evil, materialism, and a disregard for our neighbor. When obstacles disrupt our paths to the dreams we hold dear, the Gospel of John reminds us to embrace the light of Jesus and follow Plan A. We will be tested by obstacles. When we surmount our obstacles, we signal to God that we have faith.

✝ ✝ ✝

Through Faith We Receive the Grace of God

I love the snow. As I was getting ready to shovel, for the last time, the driveway of the house we had just sold and lived in for seventeen years, I thought about why I loved shoveling in the emerging light of early morning. It is a time when I can be alone in my mind. The systematic process of shoveling snow inspires my thoughts. I am alone in the stillness, surrounded by pure white. I am bundled up and warm, and I know my driveway well. I know where to start and how to finish. This rhythm allows me to reflect on God. I connect the events of my life and silently pray and am thankful.

I am glad to do this task that helps my family. When they wake up, the cars are cleared out and they can safely go about their day. Both my parental and husbandly instincts are satisfied. I take pride in making everything just right. I work hard to do the best job. I ask, *"Is this the way Jesus would want me to do it?"* And when I finish, I rest and look at my good work. I make the sign of the cross and move toward the house. My work is done.

Buried deep in the New Testament is a seldom-cited verse: *"But someone will say, 'You have faith and I have works.' Show me your faith apart from your works, and by my works I will show you my faith."* (James 2:18) We venture into the Gospels. Talk about the mighty writings of Paul. We recite and memorize the Psalms, but this little verse contains both the assurance of faith and its outcome. Through faith we receive the grace of God. It manifests itself in our good works for others. This grace is bestowed upon us from God without merit. With this grace and faith, we work, and our works become a reflection of this faith and grace.

Over the centuries many wars have been fought over whether it is through grace that we are saved or through works. Martin Luther believed salvation comes only through grace. Others say it is only by way of our works. This question became one of the major tenets of the great Protestant revolt. But two things are clear: we are given unmerited grace through faith, and faith inspires our good work.

✝ ✝ ✝

Childlike Trust in the Unseen

The development of faith requires hard work and a childlike trust in the unseen. Some arrive easily, but for most, faith is developed over time. Our faith is not like a book that we read and then put on a shelf. It is an everyday attitude. Each day, our faith will be tested. Sometimes with little events and other times with big events. We will both succeed and fail. We should never give in to the belief that *"we did not have enough faith."* We should instead persist.

The valleys of our lives are periods of preparation to see the unseen. Our God is not a condemning God, but a loving God. The world might tell us otherwise. Our relationship with God is deeply personal and intimate. Others will try to help, and we should listen and assess what they say. However, in the end, our individual faith is special and only owned by us. With God, we steer our own canoe of faith. This faith we acquire is a healing faith for all the times of our lives.

CHAPTER 2

PRAYER AND LISTENING FOR THE WIND

"Pray then in this way: Our father in heaven, hallowed be your name. Your kingdom come. Your will be done, on earth as it is in heaven. Give us this day our daily bread. And forgive us our debts, as we also have forgiven our debtors. And do not bring us to the time of trial but rescue us from the evil one."

—MATTHEW 6:9–13

The Lord's Prayer

While I was discussing prayer with a friend of mine, Les, he related to me his morning practice. Each morning on his bike ride, he would recite the Lord's Prayer. Previously, he had struggled with how to pray and what to pray for. He discovered the Lord's Prayer while reading the Sermon on the Mount in the Gospel of Matthew and noted that this was Jesus's example of prayer. So, he began to incorporate the prayer into his morning bike ride and later would also say it at other quiet times of the day. Over time he began to feel that he was just reciting the lines and not being sincere. He began to change the words to reflect his understanding of the Lord's Prayer. For instance, instead of saying "our father in heaven," he would replace it with "God our creator" or something similar. Or instead of saying "give us this day our daily bread," he would say, "Feed me your words of wisdom." This kept the prayer fresh for my friend and helped him explore his relationship with God.

The Lord's Prayer appears twice in the Bible: first in Matthew 6:9–13 and then in a shorter form in Luke 11:2–4. The version in Matthew is part of the famous Sermon on the Mount. In Luke, Jesus uses the prayer to explain to his disciples how to pray. In both cases it contains the elements that are important in a prayer. First is praising and recognizing the sovereign nature of God. This is followed by petition. There are three petitions in the Lord's Prayer. The first is for the substance to live a godly life: *"Give us this day our daily bread."* This can mean food, spiritual guidance, or personal strength. The second is asking God to *"forgive us our debts,"* or sins, and that's followed quickly by our taking responsibility for forgiving our neighbor's debts or sins. The third petition is for protection. Protection from evil, but also from the temptations of evil. Over time the prayer has morphed into longer forms that place further emphasis on the sovereign nature of God. For instance, many endings add something along the lines of *"for yours is the kingdom, the power, and the glory forever more."* The verse quoted at the top of this chapter is a direct quote from the NKJV Bible.

Many of us struggle with how, what, and when to pray. *Jesus gives us the Lord's Prayer as a basic prayer that will open up our prayer-life.* In our busy lives, this prayer is easily memorized and can be said

> *"Jesus gives us the Lord's Prayer as a basic prayer that will open up our prayer-life."*

many times during the quiet periods of the day. The prayer is extraordinarily adaptable to our personal circumstances. My friend Les learned how to adapt the prayer with creativity and tailored it to his day. God does not want us to just say the prayer from memory; God wants our prayers to be from the heart and to be part of our personal relationship with Him. It is, therefore, okay to use the Lord's Prayer as a template and expand it to fit into our own connection with God. Following the parameters of the Lord's Prayer and remembering to conclude with "in Jesus' name I pray" were the two things Les needed in his prayer-life to help him with his personal relationship with God.

✞   ✞   ✞

Developing Faith Through Continuous Prayer

Prayer is an essential part of developing a strong faith. Through prayer we converse with the sacred and begin a dialogue with God about our life. We will either hear or see responses. At first there might not appear to be answers, but over time they are revealed through the events of our lives as we move deeper in our relationship with God. Our prayer-life expands, and we stretch out the boundaries of prayer.

As we go deeper, prayer becomes a regular part of our day, our faith is strengthened. We also begin to broaden the context of our prayers, leading to a richer prayer and faith-life. There are four elements of prayer that can be said as individual prayers or, in many cases, included together in a single prayer. They are:

- **Prayer of Adoration to God**. This element reflects our faith in God and the sovereign nature of God. It is also a praising of God. In the Lord's Prayer, we see it expressed as *"hallowed be thy name."*

- **Prayer of Petition.** This is where we request and ask for God's help. Simple words expressing our needs. In the Lord's Prayer, we see this expressed as *"give us our daily bread."*

- **Prayer of Intercession.** It is here we are being a good neighbor and moving from ourselves to others. We are asking for life assistance for a neighbor. We are asking God to intercede on behalf of our neighbor. In the verse *"give us our daily bread,"* by using the word "us" we are not only asking for ourselves, but also for our neighbor. Prayers of intercession that stand alone usually contain a more direct request to aid our neighbor.

- **Prayer of Thankfulness.** This element of prayer is when we take the time to thank God for his involvement in our lives and reflects our gratitude for all that God has done for us. Perhaps this is as a result of a prayer that has been answered or a favorable event where we are sure God was present.

God wants us to pray with our hearts. Accomplishing this requires an emptying of our thoughts or emerging into a state where we are uniquely alone with God. This is a place that soothes us and frees our minds for this sacred conver-

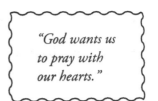

"God wants us to pray with our hearts."

sation, centering ourselves to be focused only on God. It is our heart that God wants, free of daily tasks and to-do lists. Many people find a quiet, comfortable place to pray, a routine in the morning that takes them away from the rest of the world.

A friend of mine, Dana, came to me saying, *"I feel guilty when I pray."*

"Why?" I asked.

"Because I use rosary beads to pray," Dana said.

"Do you feel God hears you?"

"Yes."

"Are the answers you receive personal and unique to you?"

"They are," Dana replied. *"But why is praying with rosary beads considered idol worship?"*

I replied, *"It isn't as long as they aren't what you are praying to."*

I could tell the rosary helped Dana to get into a deeper state of prayer, and they were her way of cleansing her mind to hear God. It was a comfortable spot that allowed her to be open to God's words.

God wants us to be in prayer continuously, and God wants to hear our desires. Being overly prescriptive with our prayer-life can make it rigid and meaningless. There are only a few guidelines that I can offer to people who ask me how to pray:

- As it is in the Lord's Prayer, I suggest always starting with a praising of God. In this statement we recognize the sovereignty of God.

- Always treat prayer as a sacred act.

- Ensure that you are in a place and mindset that will be free of distractions.

- Pray through Jesus and recognize the redeeming aspect of Jesus.

- Pray truthfully—God knows the truth about us already!

✟ ✟ ✟

Staying Focused While Praying

In theological school, we all had to take a class on prayer. We would practice prayer in each class. Over the course of a few days, I began to hear the term "monkey brain" used by my classmates. My classmates used the term to describe the mind wandering while they were praying. When I first heard this expression, I was very relieved that my classmates experienced the same drifting of the mind during their prayer time as I did. It happens to all of us, but for a long time I thought it was just me.

In prayer class, thoughts other than our prayers would enter our minds, and we had to force ourselves to return to God. The mind's wandering was always an indication that we had not set ourselves enough apart from the world. We still had not emptied ourselves and were not really engaged in conversation with God. But "monkey brain" happens to all who pray, and when it does, we must return to God in an empty state. Sometimes it serves as a quiet reminder of where we are, or an indication that we are not in uninterruptable state. But because prayer is sacred, we must return emptied.

Charles L. Allen, a mid-twentieth-century author and pastor, describes prayer as follows: *Fundamental to prayer is a sense of need that we ourselves cannot meet, and faith that God is both able and willing to meet that need.* When we search for something to meet our needs, we search in many places. We search at work, in our relationships, and in our readings. The more we search, the more we seem to miss what we're looking for. Going directly to God through prayer will open us to His desires for us and, when we are patient and faithful, God will reveal the answers we seek.

✟ ✟ ✟

Faithful Prayer Is the Recognition That God Is the Source of Our Strength

Jesus tells us to pray with the following attitude: *"Whatever you ask for in prayer with faith, you will receive."* (Matthew 21:22) In this verse Jesus tells us to pray with faith. A faith that our prayer will be answered. A faith that we will watch the events of our lives respond to our requests. A faith that our thankfulness is pointed to God. With this faith, we will receive. The desire to receive is not based on ego, but on a spirit-led connectedness. We might receive a message that is very contrary to our deep desires. With faith, we should accept this answer from God as our path. This moment of wondering how and why God responded is a critical step in developing a powerfully productive prayer-life.

✝ ✝ ✝

Connecting Our Prayers with the Bible

There are many times Jesus prays in the Gospels. In the Garden of Gethsemane, while in the desert, and early in the morning. In his prayers, Jesus is showing us how to be in dialogue with God. He is also teaching us that prayer is valuable in searching for answers and examining our heart. Many times we will receive God's advice or answer through a verse we read in the Bible. At first these answers may seem very random, but through careful observation we will find what we seek.

Our prayer-life connected to the Bible is the single most important influencer in developing a strong faith and a personal relationship with Jesus. With our prayers and Bible readings, we do three things:

- Recognize the sovereign nature of God.

- Reveal our intimate thoughts to God.

- Hear the voice of God in response.

When we pray, we have immediately recognized God as sovereign, just by praying. We are saying to God, *We want you in our life; we are striving for answers to the issues in our lives, and we are acknowledging in the very act of prayer that God can give us solutions and guidance.*

During prayer we reveal to God our thoughts, concerns, and desires with a level of intimacy that is seldom shared with others. We reveal things that would make us uncomfortable in human interactions. These thoughts are very personal, but they are truths about us that God already knows. In a healthy state of prayer all is revealed.

In the deepest part of our prayers, God will sometimes speak back through a verse. We will have thoughts that were not ours at the beginning of our prayer. We will wonder where they came from. These thoughts may appear to be random but contain the beginning of God's answer. Perhaps in the form of a readjustment to our point of view. Perhaps a reframing of what we really want and need. Perhaps even a reduction in the intensity of our prayer, pointing toward a new way of thinking. Learning to decipher what is random and what is real in these responses is an important part of our prayer-life. The more we pray and study the Bible, the more we see and hear God in our lives. Our faith becomes strengthened.

✟ ✟ ✟

The Different States of Our Existence

Famed scholar Walter Brueggemann says, *"Prayer is a great antidote to the illusion that we are self-made."* Brueggemann also describes our prayer-life as occurring in three possible states:

- **A State of Orientation.** It is in this state when all is right with the world. The state of our being is thankful, and it is from here where prayers of gratitude are derived.

- **A State of Disorientation.** In this state our lives have been disrupted and chaos exists. We are not sure where to turn or how we can move forward. This is a state where prayers of petition occur.

- **A State of Reorientation.** It is here where we have emerged from the valley of despair, and the light of dawn shows up in our life. A place where we see resolution and hope returns. Prayers of praise and thanks occur in this state.

Specifically, Brueggemann associates these states of expression to the largest book in the Bible, the Psalms. The Psalms represent the prayers of our ancestors from the ancient past. A collection of poem-like prayers that extend back as far as Moses and span a period of one thousand years, many attributed to King David. In them are expressions of all three life states. Some include all three states and some only one or two of the three.

In reading the Book of Psalms and its 150 chapters, you hear the ancient prayers. You will feel the writers' current life status, be it thankfulness, concerned, or relieved. The Psalms are a wonderful resource to read and experience the feelings of

YOUR FAITH HAS MADE YOU WELL

ancient writers from the past. If you read only five a day, you can finish this section of the Bible in a month, and there is no better way to supplement our prayer-lives than to connect them with scripture. Through this daily combination, our lives move from being random events to being a connected set of providential circumstances.

✟ ✟ ✟

Hearing the Spiritual Winds of God

Early in the Gospel of John, Jesus talks with Nicodemus, a member of the ruling elite in Jerusalem. Nicodemus has come to Jesus late in the evening with a compelling desire to know more about him and his purpose. To explain faith and the Spirit, Jesus tells Nicodemus, *"The wind blows where it chooses, and you hear the sound of it, but you do not know where it comes from or where it goes. So, it is with everyone who is born of the Spirit."* (John 3:8)

I met Wendy Paige at Drew Theological School. She is a tall and powerful black minister with an up-front spirit, exceedingly friendly and enthusiastic, and a wonderful orator of the Christian faith. Her prayer-life was a constant and relied-upon asset in her life.

She came to me one day to ask about coincidences that were happening in her life. *"Do you have them?"* she asked. I said, *"All the time."* She then asked how I knew it was God speaking to me and responding to my prayers through these coincidences. I replied, *"I'm a math person, so I use the laws of probability to discern. If it happens once it could be a coincidence, but when it happens many times it is the Spirit of God."* These moments of apparent coincidence were common to both of us.

Wendy prayed frequently, and often she would get an answer. An answer that was usually better than she had

> *"The Spirit spoke with her, because she spoke with the Spirit."*

expected. And sometimes an answer that was revealed in a way so unusual that it was startling. People would tell her that such an answer was just a coincidence. However, the events continued, and they filled her faith. Her question to me was one of confirmation. She already knew the answer: these events were the Spirit talking and responding to her prayers. The Spirit spoke with her because she spoke with the Spirit, and she knew the answers were the sound of the wind of God. Her experiences over time overwhelmed the outside world's knowledge. The physical world could not explain these events, other than to say they were coincidences.

Near the end of the dialogue with Nicodemus, Jesus explains this phenomenon by comparing it to the wind. He says that when we live with the Spirit, we see God at work. We see His influence in our lives. We see that events are not just random but a well-crafted reply to our prayers. We begin to expect this kind of response. We begin to interpret these events not as our desired answers, but as reflecting God's desire for us. They will be unusual and very personal. Answers that we can intimately recognize. Answers that are so extraordinary and intimate they defy the laws of probability.

Wendy felt the wind. She felt it because she answered the compelling voice of the Spirit. She continuously prayed and engaged in a spiritual dialogue—a deep and rich dialogue with God. Her heart was ready for answers, and they appeared. Maybe through a random Bible verse. Or maybe through an innocent conversation. Or even maybe brought by an unexpected visitor. The answers were always unusual, deeply personal, and responsive. They were real for Wendy and, connected together over time, defied the laws of probability. The coincidences became overwhelmed by math.

✞   ✞   ✞

The Silent Answers Are from God

Prayers are not always answered with ringing bells or flashes of light. For instance, the great prophet Elijah was waiting for an answer to his prayers and heard the sheer silence of God, described in 1 Kings as: *"Go out and stand on the mountain before the Lord'* . . . *and after the earthquake a fire, but the Lord was not in the fire; and after the fire a sound of sheer silence."* (1 Kings 19:11–12)

A friend of mine, Bob, was in the process of selling an important asset. The sale would be a crucial part of his future and success. Bob was determined to be a good seller—to not hide anything from the buyer and to provide them with a product that exceeded expectations. Bob responded faithfully to all of the buyer's requests and went further than his lawyer or broker expected him to go, but the requests did not end. After each obstacle was resolved, another popped up. A meeting was scheduled between all the parties to find a clear path to resolution.

The day before the meeting, Bob's wife announced that the doctor had found something during her checkup that required a radiologist's opinion. The appointment with the radiologist was scheduled at the same time as my friend's important meeting. His wife told him to go to the meeting, and she would be okay. Bob felt besieged. *How can I ignore my wife? But how can I secure our future?* He prayed throughout the day. He prayed for God to give him the wisdom to make the right decisions with his business and to help his wife. He went to the meeting, and his wife went to the radiologist.

During the meeting, there were many questions. Tough questions. My friend answered them all honestly. At one point, the broker for the buyer became unrelenting. Bob felt a spirit of resolve fall over him, and he became quietly serious. Normally Bob's mannerisms were friendly and engaging, but now he became dead serious. Looking firmly into the eyes of the buyer's broker and without hesitation, he stated firmly and in a quiet tone, "If there is a problem, I will pay to have it resolved. It is what I have done to this point and will continue to do." He left the meeting concerned about his wife and at the same time about the state of this important sale.

> "While Bob had waited in silence, God had answered his prayers."

At home, he sat in his favorite chair and waited in silence. A short time passed, and he received a call. The broker said, "It is done. You have done everything and have no more to do. The sale is going forward." Very shortly after, his wife called and told him that the radiologist had found nothing serious, and she would need only some minor medical attention. A wave of joy overcame him. While Bob had waited in silence, God had answered his prayers. No great bell was rung; there were no fireworks. The quiet winds of life had brought his answer. Life was in balance.

✟ ✟ ✟

Praying Thankfully

Many of our prayers are prayers of petition in that we are asking something of God. To have a fully balanced prayer-life, prayers of thanksgiving are important as well. With God and loved ones alike, always asking and not thanking leads to unhealthy relationships. Quiet prayers of thankfulness are the recognition of where our gifts and blessings come from. This reminds me of a brief conversation I had with a close friend a few years ago.

On the Wednesday before Thanksgiving, I called a business owner I knew, Vicki, to share some information. After, I asked her what she was doing for the holiday. She replied, *"I am going to take the remainder of the day off and do nothing but rest tomorrow. I have had a good fall season, and I want to just be thankful."* In her voice I heard relief. She had worked hard, harder than most. She had endured some tough times as she started her business, and now she finally knew she was going to make it.

How many of us have had that moment when the world seems right? That moment when we have done all we could. Thankfulness comes in that moment when we reflect on the climb we have overcome. It is a brief resting spot to give thanks and remember where we have been. For Vicki, that Thanksgiving was her moment. She had worked incredibly hard. Along the way, she'd had her doubters, but she stayed focused on her goal and plowed ahead. She maintained the wonderful balance between taking care of her customers and running a successful business. Thanksgiving Day was a time for satisfaction that she had passed the test. For that moment, she was oriented with life.

Sitting back in these moments is also the time to reflect on the wondrous deeds of God—how He stands with us as we struggle up our personal mountains. God hears our prayers, and when we comply with God's wishes, God rewards us. In Jeremiah 29:11 it says, *"For surely, I know the plans I have for you, says the Lord, plans for your welfare and not for harm, to give you a future with hope."*

> "God, our creator, has many plans and a rich life in store for us."

God is with us in our darkest moments of struggle. God reveals to us our path and seeps into our hearts. As we listen, God becomes an easy mentor. God, our creator, has many plans and a rich life in store for us. When we look up to the sky at night, we see the wondrous inheritance of God's creation.

We have many days to be thankful for the fruits of our work. Maybe today is a day to be thankful for God's partnership. Maybe today is a day of rest. Maybe today is a day to reflect on our past and future with God.

✟ ✟ ✟

Truthful Prayer Strengthens Our Partnership with God

Prayers are our way of talking with God through Jesus. They are our way of creating and growing a stronger personal relationship with God. Over time it becomes a deep, mutual partnership in our lives. As with any relationship, we must approach it with complete honesty. For this relationship to become strong, a high degree of mutuality and truth must be present. The relationship with God is sacred. Jesus tells us, ***"God is spirit, and those who worship him must worship in spirit and truth."*** (John 4:24)

If we want to have reliable relationships, they must come from a spirit of being truthful. So it is with God as well. When we communicate with God, our goal

> "Being truthful strengthens our partnership with God."

should be taking responsibility for our actions and being truthful. Being truthful strengthens our partnership with God. Our mirror is then always pointed to ourselves. However, when we simply deflect difficult conversations back to God, we are not really searching for the truth; we are searching for an easy way out of our challenges.

When we pray, truthful admissions help our prayers. When we only point our problems back to God, we disrupt the relationship. Sure, God wants to hear our anguish, joys, and concerns, but God also wants us to be a partner. God has plans for us that require our active involvement.

Prayer-life is the essential part of building faith. It requires daily persistence, patience, and truthfulness. No one's faith can be built without these ingredients. Prayer that is Biblically based will be fundamentally sound. Prayers are our direct line to God through Jesus. We will see answers, not in only in human terms, but through miraculous events that are so extraordinary and personal we know they are from God. We will move from seeing things as random to an answer from God. Through a productive prayer-life our faith is strengthened, and we are healed through our continuous dialogue with God.

CHAPTER 3

WHAT SORT OF MAN IS THIS?

"They were amazed, saying, 'What sort of man is this, that even the winds and the sea obey him?'"

—Matthew 8:27

Faith in Jesus Means Not Being Afraid

Jesus is sleeping in the cargo hold of a boat that also contains his disciples. From seemingly nowhere, the wind picks up, and the seas begin to roil. The waves become so large that they threaten to swamp the boat. The disciples begin to panic. Trembling, they awake Jesus and with terror in their voices say, *"Lord save us! We are perishing."* Jesus arises and rebukes the disciples by saying, ***"Why are you afraid, you of little faith?"*** Immediately, Jesus stops the wind and calms the sea. Upon seeing this, the disciples say, *"What sort of man is this, that even the winds and the sea obey him?"*

An amazing part of this story is the lack of faith of the disciples. By now they had witnessed healings and other miracles performed by Jesus. They had seen demons cast out, had heard the wonderful Sermon on the Mount, and seen destitute lives changed. We can well wonder, how could they still doubt that they would be saved from the sea? How had they let their human fears override their knowledge of who Jesus was? We in turn can wonder, would we be different?

Jesus replies with, ***"Why are you afraid, you of little faith?"*** (Matthew 8:26) His reply contains a universal message about the difficulty of faith. Despite all they had seen from Jesus, those with him still allowed their worldly fears to swamp their faith. Just as with us, despite all we have seen from Jesus, we sometimes allow our faith to do the same. Each time Jesus visits us we are left with amazement—many times wondering why we doubted.

Also, in this story is a universal question of *"What sort of man is this?"* Who is Jesus that he calms the wind and seas? Who is Jesus that we can have confidence in him as our savior? While the heavenly answer to these questions exceeds humankind's understanding, we are shown on a regular basis Jesus's value to humankind. We are told to have faith, because we should. This is easy to say, but a simple platitude is not enough. Faith, in part, is experiencing and knowing *"what sort of man this is."*

✝ ✝ ✝

Jesus Is God

Returning to when Nicodemus approached Jesus to discover who he was, as discussed in the last chapter, Nicodemus was part of the ruling Sanhedrin. The Sanhedrin consisted of seventy men who helped the Romans rule Judea during Jesus's time. Jesus had been making waves and, in many ways, had started to become a problem for the local ruling authorities. Nicodemus had come to discover for himself *"what sort of man this was"* and had come late at night so as not to be seen by others. An ember of yearning burned in Nicodemus. A yearning to be closer to God. He was on a mission of discovery.

Nicodemus knew Jesus was special, despite his compatriots' desire to have Jesus silenced. Nicodemus could not see their way so quickly. Something was unusual about this man. Perhaps something divine. Sensing this, Jesus says to Nicodemus, *"For God so loved the world that he gave his only Son, so that everyone who believes in him may not perish but may have eternal life."* (John 3:16) This statement by Jesus is perhaps the most widely quoted verse in the Bible. A familiar verse with very far-reaching meanings.

Many of us have seen people holding up signs that say, *"John 3:16."* We have seen the sign at the World Series, at the Masters, at all-star games, and on street corners. The verse has long been held up as the principle statement of Jesus's purpose. For some, this message has been associated with overly zealous people, and for others, it has been seen as an enduring statement of faith, but this statement is more than just a Christian slogan.

> *"When we look at this statement with this revelation, it expands who Jesus is to us. He is God."*

Jesus is making this statement about himself. This was not a pronouncement by a well-known leader or religious scholar—it came directly from him. This verse was said by Jesus about who he was.

In today's society we view it superficially, almost like a slogan for advertising, but a more careful examination reveals that this is a critical Biblical statement and not just a statement of allegiance or a rallying cry for two billion people that shows up in familiar places like sporting events. Hidden in this statement is an important clue to answering the question *what sort of man is this?* It states nothing less than that Jesus is God. When we read this verse in the Bible, we see that the word "*Son*" is capitalized. Inspired by God, the translators of this ancient text always capitalized any word in the Bible that refers to God. "*Son*" is capitalized in this statement because Jesus is referring to himself as God. When we look at this statement with this revelation, it expands who Jesus is to us. He is God.

Jesus is God. God is revealing Himself to the world. Revealing God's values and expectations. Revealing God's purpose and God's purpose for humankind. A revelation that God is with all humankind. A generous gift for all humankind, whom we ourselves have been created in the image of God. A revealing of the values that God wants us to live by. A revealing of our purpose, to love God and love our neighbor. A revealing that through believing in the Son, we will have eternal life. This revelation also extends beyond just a life of eternity. It extends to a way of life that, when followed, provides eternal peace and our own healing. It reveals a life of confidence that our lives and purpose matter.

John 3:16 reveals who Jesus was—a wonderful present for all of humankind. Many Christians spin off into different directions when we try to describe Jesus. We have our theories and we have our arguments. Some think he was a great teacher, and he was. Some think he was the "*Lamb of God,*" and he was. Some think he is our Redeemer, and he is. Scholars spend years developing theories and describing single aspects of Christ. Ultimately, Jesus is many things, and a complete list is undefinable by any human. Jesus is all of the things we labor to describe and much more. Jesus is God. And he is God's gift and revealer for humankind.

> *"Jesus is God. And he is God's gift and revealer for humankind.*

We find further evidence of this assertion in the very first lines of the Gospel of John. These first lines also explain the substance and presence of Jesus: *"In the beginning was the Word, and the Word was with God, and the Word was God."* (John 1:1)

Three critical statements are made in this first sentence of the Gospel of John that confirm Jesus's identity, from creation to today. Understanding these statements helps us understand Jesus's mission and Jesus's existence with and *as* God. The Gospel of John is the last of the four Gospels and was written in the late first century or potentially early in the second century. Its original language was ancient Greek, and in turn it is expressed in a very philosophical manner.

In the first statement, *"In the beginning was the Word,"* we notice that *"Word"* is capitalized. As stated before, when the Bible uses a capital letter, this indicates it is God. The Gospel uses the word *"Word"* as a reference to Jesus. *"Word"* is used to describe Jesus and further asserts that Jesus existed in the beginning. The statement *"In the beginning"* has a direct connection to Genesis 1:1, *"In the beginning God created . . ."* From this statement in John, we can conclude that Jesus existed at the beginning of creation and was the agent of creation.

The second statement, *"and the Word was with God,"* tells us that Jesus coexists with God. Jesus participated in creation, not in an inferior position, but as part of creation. In the deep ocean of the divine, the substance of God is partially disclosed. This powerful statement expresses the partnership and coexistence of Jesus with God. This statement also expresses the eternal communion of Jesus with God.

> *"Jesus participated in creation, not in an inferior position, but as part of creation."*

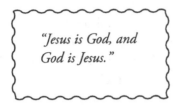

"Jesus is God, and God is Jesus."

The third statement, *"and the Word was God,"* makes the statement that Jesus was God. This final turning of the covers unveils the reality that Jesus is God and God is Jesus. A body with three substances, when we include the Holy Spirit. An eternal, divine being that works through creation, the past, and the future. Jesus is not defined as a creature independent of God, but as God.

The fact is that Jesus is God and not just a missionary to humankind. Jesus was an agent of creation and is the Alpha and Omega. Through Jesus, God is revealed to the world. Jesus both saves and reveals. This concept of revelation is critical to understanding the *"Word."* Jesus is many things beyond just a redeemer. Jesus existed at the beginning and is part of the trinity that is God.

✝ ✝ ✝

Jesus the Forgiver

Now that we can accept and believe Jesus was and is with God, we can understand many aspects of Jesus's value to and for humankind. For instance, during the Last Supper, Jesus provides the words to the apostles of a communion with him—a joining with Jesus in the resurrection and a new life. The words offer hope of a forgiveness of our sins and a repeated life of a second chance when we connect our hearts with God. When Jesus raised his cup to the apostles and said, ***"Drink from it, all of you; for this is my blood of the covenant, which is poured out for many for the forgiveness of sins."*** (Matthew 26:27–28) In this invitation, we see a loving God and not a condemning God, a forgiveness poured out for us.

One of my clients, Chuck, lost his job and expressed to me his frustration that he felt he once again had let Jesus down. He believed that Jesus had put him in a spot to get the job he wanted and in losing it he had failed Jesus. His self-esteem took a big hit. Chuck had done nothing wrong. He'd tried to help his company, became a victim of circumstance, and was released. However, over and over in his mind he wondered, *What if I had done this? Perhaps I should have done that.* His feeling that he had let Jesus down was the darkest part of his remorse, a sense of failure that was complete and deep. He felt God had given him a chance at a great career, and he had blown it.

Chuck wondered if Jesus would forgive him. He promised he would do better next time. He prayed for a second chance. I reminded him of the covenant he had with Jesus. I reminded him that what Jesus offers is the essence of love, greater than the love of a parent for a child. As a lifelong believer, Chuck knew all these things, but this was personal. Alone with his thoughts, he could not shake the sense of failure. All he wanted was a second chance.

We need look no further than apostle Peter to see the attitude of forgiveness and love that Jesus has for humankind. After being taught to walk on water with faith, Peter failed. He was usually the voice for the other eleven when they consistently failed to understand the messages of Jesus. In a complete act of failure, Peter denied Jesus three times on the fateful night before the crucifixion. Peter had a long history of failures, but Jesus held firm in his commitment and called Peter **"the rock upon which I will build my church."** As we know, after Jesus's resurrection and ascension, Peter became the leader of the group that carried forward the messages of Jesus.

Chuck called me on a Monday after he found out the bad news, and we talked for a long time. He went back and forth between despair and hope. Intellectually, he knew Jesus was with him, but emotionally he could not shake the sense of failure. He prayed constantly that day.

The following morning, after a difficult night of sleep, he rose to find a message on his phone. A company wanted to hire him. A job that would pay him more. A job that was better suited for who he was. A job that reminded him that Jesus was with him.

With Jesus, when we have a repentant heart, we have a life of second chances. A life that unfurls Jesus's majesty. A life that, when approached with Jesus at its center, reveals his love and forgiveness. All of us will fail, but when we look to Jesus we are lifted back up to a life of completeness.

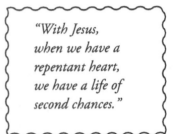

"With Jesus, when we have a repentant heart, we have a life of second chances."

✟ ✟ ✟

Jesus Walked Many Miles to Be with Humankind

Another aspect of Jesus was his desire to be with humankind. In the Gospel of Matthew, describing the early days of Jesus's mission on earth, the verse says, *"Jesus went throughout Galilee, teaching in their synagogues and proclaiming the good news of the kingdom and curing every disease and every sickness among the people."* (Matthew 4:23)

In reading this verse, we get another glimmer of the essence of Jesus. He did not sit at a desk by himself. He went out and visited people. He cured the sick and taught others. This model of walking around, helping, and visiting is a lesson of how our faith heals us. As images of God, to be whole, we should reach out and be with people.

> *"We are all made
> in the image of
> God and are the
> children of God."*

I have found that we some-times spend too much time in our "inner castles." During my counseling work, I often meet with individuals who express feelings of despondency and dejection. They might lament, *"I had such an awful week!"* They wonder aloud, *"What's wrong with me?"* or *"Why do I fail so often?"* When I dig deeper, trying to get at the heart of their feelings and worries, I often find that they're spending too much time alone with their thoughts. It is very easy, if we spend too much time alone, to dwell on negative thoughts or feelings; we use these thoughts to beat ourselves up. As a rule, it is never good to call yourself names. We are all made in the image of God and are the chil-dren of God.

Also, we are wise to be careful with whom we do spend time. There are those who support us and those who promote negative feelings. Generally, successful people surround them-selves with positive influencers. Positive people lift us up and become mirrors of life to follow.

Sure, Jesus would sometimes go off to quiet places to pray and meditate away from others, but most of the time he was among the people. His ministry involved dining with others, walking to distant towns to meet as many people as he could, offering spiritual guidance, and curing the sick. Quite simply, Jesus exists to serve, love, and support others.

As images of God, we should spend time with others as well. When we interact with others, we receive an elixir—an affirmation that we exist and matter. When we look someone in the eye and ask, *"How is your day?"* we are validating them and ourselves as well. Every positive interaction with others reminds us that we are good in God's eyes and worthy of his love. When we ask people about themselves and then truly listen to their responses, we connect with them, allowing them to share their dreams and worries. We give them a voice, and we make them feel heard and loved. In doing so, we become more joyful and energized. When we are with others and give the gift of listening and caring, we model ourselves as the image of God.

I often say in my sessions that people like people who like people. At first this may sound self-serving. Should you only be kind to others because you want them to like you? No, of course not, but if we are sincere in our affection and regard for others, we forge a mutual bond that

"God wants us among people. He created us to share our lives with others."

offers shared benefits. By being with people, we help affirm and we are affirmed.

When Jesus walked among others, his mission was not only to heal and to proclaim the "good news," but also simply to be with others—to offer companionship and love. Our inner castles are good places to rest and pray, but we can only stay for a while. God wants us among people. He created us to share our lives with others.

✟　✟　✟

Taking the Yoke of Jesus

Jesus tells us, ***"Take my yoke upon you and learn from me; for I am gentle and humble in heart, and you will find rest for your souls."*** (Matthew 11:29) It is a simple request to turn away from those things that distract us and turn to accepting the lessons and wisdom of Jesus. To have faith in Jesus rights our path, not only because he is with us, but because we pick up his ways.

My friend Mel, who had left the corporate world to help the poor for the Catholic Church in the northwest part of the United States but had now returned, called me in distress. He had walked away from a well-paying job for two years to help those less fortunate. Upon his return to the corporate world, he was finding it hard to find a new job. Many interviewers did not understand why he left, and many were put off by the fact that he was sixty. He kept meeting dead ends in his job search. Confusion about doing good in the world and then being rebuffed in the job market had created a crisis in his life. He did not need a job for the money; he just wanted to belong again.

> "His self-esteem plummeted, and he began to feel worthless. His searching kept leading him to disappointment."

Over the next two years, Mel searched for a place to work. He prayed on a regular basis. He even went away for a week to a retreat center looking for his answer. He wanted desperately to belong again. His self-esteem plummeted, and he began to feel worthless. His search kept leading him to disappointment.

We talked on a weekly basis, and during these sessions, I would often ask why a job in his old world was so important. He would reply, *"Because it is my identity."* For years he had worked hard to provide for his family and build a wonderful résumé, but now that he had lost that ability he felt he was also losing his identity.

✝ ✝ ✝

During these two years, Mel still helped others. In fact, he helped a group of nuns create a shelter for homeless pregnant woman. Many days, he put in long hours painting and fixing the shelter. Within this community he found acceptance, but not what he wanted. He wanted to go back to his old life. Oftentimes, I told him how much I admired his compassionate and charitable efforts for others. I relayed that when I told his story to other people, they were amazed at his giving nature and life. But this was still not enough for Mel. He kept searching and not finding. Eventually, he decided to go back to school and become an EMT while he waited for a more ideal new job. He kept waiting for Jesus to answer his prayer of finding him a job.

Typical of Mel, he was one of the best students in the EMT training. Despite some physical limitations, he was able to keep up with the younger people in his class. He began to thrive. Many times, I would get a text from him saying something like: *I can't talk tonight, I am going out with my classmates.* I was used to this, as many of the people I help eventually find their answer and move on to their new life. It is a very familiar process. I miss these people and often wonder how they are doing, but my job was done.

Later, in one of our final conversations, Mel told me that he had prayed for an answer many times, but he kept looking in the wrong spots. His identity did not lie in his place in the old corporate world but in helping make the world a better

> *"Jesus had been answering his prayers; he just had not paid attention."*

place. Jesus had been answering his prayers; he just had not paid attention.

Jesus asks us to take his yoke. Jesus reminds us that he is *"gentle and humble of heart,"* and that his *"yoke is light."* How many times do we pray for something that we want, but Jesus gives us something different? He gives us a life plan that soothes our soul and gives us meaning. Many times, it is about following a new path, away from the familiar. A path of uncertainty on which we take his yoke and are guided by his *"gentle and humble"* heart.

Mel is peaceful now, and I miss our weekly calls, but I'm happy that Mel's new identity is on a path of giving. When we ask ourselves, *"What sort of man is this?"* Jesus's answer is also that he is *"gentle and humble of heart."*

✠ ✠ ✠

Jesus Sees No Differences in Race, Gender, or Class

Jesus showed no partiality to those he hung out with. He knew no bias. He was the original diversity champion. For some in the ancient world this caused a problem, and in the Gospel of Luke it says, *"All who saw it began to grumble and said, 'He has gone to be the guest of one who is a sinner.'"* (Luke 19:7) Part of developing our faith and our own healing is expanding our circle. The very act of treating other people as equal is redemptive. Through our acceptance of all people, we emulate the acts of Jesus and live the concept that all people are made in the image of God. When we become more accepting, we also begin to satisfy the human need to help. Filling this need brings us joy.

I remember meeting Rudy Rasmus in a private room with a bishop of the United Methodist Church. He was a talker. Rudy told riveting stories about his past, his ministry, and the poor.

He was a pastor for a Methodist church in Houston, but prior to that he had run a bordello. He readily admitted that at that time he'd been living a life away from God. A life of serving himself and not his neighbor. He then came face-to-face with Jesus through a personal crisis and turned his life around. After passing his tests to become a pastor, he was given a church in one of the poorest sections of Houston. The church had only nine members. Undaunted, Rudy moved forward with this small church. In an act of pure faith and to get more people to come, he started paying one dollar to anyone who would show up at his church. Many did—the desperate, the poor, those with mental illnesses, and those who wanted to help.

Today, the church Rudy serves is over ten thousand people strong. Thirty percent of the congregants were previously homeless. Moreover, Rudy's is one of the most culturally diverse churches in the country. He attributes the success of his church to the fact that it contains a group of people who embrace the vision of tearing down the walls of classism, racism, and sexism and building bridges to experience Christ. The church feeds the poor and builds housing for the homeless through a nonprofit called the Bread of Life. The church and Rudy have changed the landscape in their part of downtown Houston. Rudy does not often preach these days; he leaves that up to the other ministers. Instead he greets attendees at the door and welcomes them to church.

In Luke 19:7, we hear people grumbling that Jesus was going to be the houseguest of a sinner. This was a frequent activity of Jesus's. He dined with sinners. He stayed at their houses. He spent his time in the Judean marketplace helping all who worked there.

> *"For Jesus and Rudy, there are no class differences, race differences, or gender differences."*

He converted women of ill repute. Jesus viewed each person as equal. Everyone was worthy of God. For Jesus and Rudy, there are no class differences, race differences, or gender differences. We are all God's people. Jesus hung out with everyone.

A friend of mine named Shari runs a nonprofit called the Hope Clinic. She serves the poor and wrestles with God, asking "why her." She goes back every day to serve, despite the potential for a life that could be more financially bountiful. She serves because she sees something many do not. Children are not poor; they are born into poverty. Addicts still need her help; where else could they go? Those without medical support need care; where else can they turn? She does not judge— she helps.

Our faith and sense of self is strengthened when we accept others. In effect, it is a healing and an expansion of our own life boundaries. By affirming others, we give them an identity and make a statement that they are worthy. In this affirmation, we also begin to create an image of ourselves as a caring person. In this caring, we affirm our own goodness as images of God. It is a bold step to dine with those who are different—a step toward our own healing. Another answer to, *"What sort of man is this?"*

✟ ✟ ✟

Jesus the Wise Advisor

Jesus certainly was a miracle maker and healer, but his words of advice are often an overlooked value in our faith. Jesus was, and is, also a great life coach. Many of the words Jesus spoke contain valuable lessons for faithful and productive living. Consider the Parable of the Weeds, in which Jesus begins explaining by saying, ***"But while everybody was asleep, an enemy came and sowed weeds among the wheat, and then*** *went away. So, when the plants came up and bore grain, then the weeds appeared as well."* (Matthew 13:25–26)

My wife and I were sitting with a receptionist who we had to schedule a routine surgical procedure with, and on the woman's head was a headset and microphone. I asked, "Why do you have your headset on?" Her reply: *"I wear it all day because I have to talk with the insurance companies all day. You might get interrupted here and there when I get a live person on the phone, so bear with me."* This woman had to call insurance companies all day regarding billing questions for the patients in the office where she worked, and many times she was put on hold for long periods of time. As she waited on hold, she served the in-person patients, and every fifteen minutes or so someone would come on the phone and ask her a quick question. She would provide the answer and get put back on hold. And so her life went, every day.

Too much of our lives are spent on hold and waiting for many minutes to get the ten-second answer we need. If it isn't the insurance company, it's the cable company or the Department of Motor Vehicles. It has become part of the American experience. These times on hold are the weeds of life. Organizations impose rules and procedures that must be followed, and we must wait on the phone or in line. In this story we see an ingenious woman who had solved the problem of the weeds in her life: wear a headset, apologize to her patients for the minor interruptions, and still get her job done. Remarkable!

In this verse, Jesus talks about the weeds of life. The parable explains that weeds

"The parable explains that weeds are always there, planted by some unknown entity that seeks to disrupt our daily routine."

are always there, planted by some unknown entity that seeks to disrupt our daily routine. When asked what we should do with the weeds, Jesus replies, in Matthew 13:30, *"Let them both grow together until the harvest."* In short, Jesus tells us to work around them. The words from Jesus are not only spiritual, but practical as well. The words of Jesus in themselves are a miracle.

✝ ✝ ✝

Following Jesus

In the opening part of this chapter, the disciples in the boat ask, *"What sort of man is this?"* They had all been around him and seen his miracles and the way crowds flocked to be with him. They'd been with him for many days and seen the many dimensions of Jesus, to the point that they could no longer fully grasp the depth and breadth of this wonderful person. Certainly, Jesus is a healer, a sage of advice, an accepting being, and a forgiver. But, most of all, he is undefinable and alone in his greatness and completeness. In a simple passage in the Book of John we see all that is required from us in knowing Jesus. It says, *"The next day Jesus decided to go to Galilee. He found Philip and said to him, 'Follow me.'"* (John 1:43)

When Henry Heinz, the founder of the H. J. Heinz Company, wrote his last will and testament, he included as his first lines, *"I desire to set forth, at the very beginning of this will, as the most important item in it, a confession of my faith in Jesus Christ as my Savior."* Henry Heinz founded the company called Heinz 57 with his brother after previously filing for bankruptcy. They started out making ketchup and eventually expanded to over sixty products. A successful company based largely in Pittsburgh, it grew to become one of the largest food-producing companies in the world. Beyond his being a devout

Christian, the unusual first words of Henry's last will and testament represented a lifetime of living his faith.

> "The words in Henry Heinz's last will and testament reflect the life he led and were a statement of his focus in following Jesus."

The H. J. Heinz Company had a reputation for fair treatment of its employees at a time when fair labor standards did not yet exist. By 1906, Henry was providing his employees with free medical care. In his facilities, he had gyms, swimming pools, and gardens. He provided educational opportunities, libraries, concerts, and lectures. He was a pioneer in safe and sanitary food preparation. At a time in our country's history when many corporations ignored these social niceties, Heinz was a leader. The words in Henry Heinz's last will and testament reflect the life he led and were a statement of his focus in following Jesus.

Jesus finds Philip and recognizes in him a stout and honest man. Philip will become one of Jesus's leading recruiters. When he meets Philip, Jesus says, *"Follow me."* Philip follows. Philip was the connection to Nathanael, Andrew, and Peter. In later life, he is credited with traveling to many parts of the Middle East and preaching the Gospel. He represented the true nature of Christianity by following Christ. Not just physically but spiritually. Following Christ requires a self-examination by ourselves, of why we follow. Do we follow for gain or profit? Or do we follow out of a real desire to know Jesus? To give up our

> "Following Christ requires a self-examination by ourselves, of why we follow."

past lives requires a change of focus. It does not mean we give up who we are and what we do, but we give up a previous focus of following ourselves and accept a focus of following Jesus. This change in focus changes our attitude about why we do things.

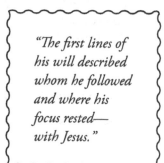

"The first lines of his will described whom he followed and where his focus rested— with Jesus."

Henry Heinz's focus could have been squeezing out a few more dollars by not being generous to his employees. He could have increased his net worth by not being charitable. However, his focus was to be successful in a way that supported his choice to follow Jesus. Certainly, his lobbying efforts for tougher food standards cost him margin dollars. But the first lines of his will described whom he followed and where his focus rested— with Jesus.

Jesus is undefinable. Some will see him as a savior, others as a redeemer. Some even view him as a sage beyond any that has walked this earth. He does have the power to heal miraculously. He does make our paths straight. No one person can ever fully capture the entire essence of Jesus, but when we have faith, we only need to follow.

What sort of man is Jesus? He is many and all things. We can debate endlessly with each other and still only touch the surface. For each person, Jesus is different, just as each of us is different.

Part Two

~

The Seasons of Faith

"The Seasons of Faith" encompasses chapters four through eleven. In these chapters we expand faith from being one person's views to many views. Life's circumstances create our faith individually, and we all enter our faith with a different perspective. Although I portray many stories and thoughts about faith, the following chapters are not intended to be prescriptive. Rather, they are meant to create an imaginative thought process in considering our own faith journey.

There are many faith stories, and all are uniquely different. Even our own entry into the Bible comes from our own life experiences. How we meet Jesus is different for everyone. This section shows the many ways we enter and acquire faith.

CHAPTER 4

I WAS BLIND, BUT NOW I SEE

"One thing I do know, that though I was blind, now I see."
—JOHN 9:25

Amazing Grace

John Newton, the former slave ship captain who wrote the famous Christian hymn "Amazing Grace," included in the lyrics words from the verse John 9:25, *"Was blind, but now I see."* On the surface, when we read the lyrics of this great song, we see a wonderful description of our Christian faith. The song's own haunting melody inspires us to feel closer to God. The most famous line, *"I was blind but now I see,"* comes directly from the story of the blind man healed by Jesus in the Gospel of John.

John Newton's past was very checkered. He had been a sailor and rose to be a skilled captain. Few could handle a ship as well as John, but he was also known for extraordinarily bad language. One sea captain considered his vocabulary the worst of any sailor's he had encountered. John frequently was disobedient, and in younger years he was punished and forced to spend time as a slave in Sierra Leone.

John was drawn to the sea. He endured numerous close calls on the ocean, where his ships were either close to sinking or in such bad weather that men were washed overboard. Even though he had led a life away from God, during these difficult moments he would still cry out, *"God have mercy."*

It was through these moments that Newton began to think about a different life—to seek a different path from the one he was on. He was discomfited shuttling innocent enslaved people from one continent to another. Disgusted with himself and his life, he sought another way.

He became associated with the early Methodist movement in England and became well known to John Wesley, its founder. Wesley saw in Newton an ember of faithful living that only needed a spark to ignite his true passion—serving his Lord. After many conversations, Wesley encouraged him to write and become a pastor. Later, Newton became a rector at a small Anglican church. While at this church, he helped write many hymns, including "Amazing Grace." Later in his life, Newton became an avowed abolitionist and was a good friend of William Wilberforce, the person largely responsible for ending the slave trade in England.

John Newton's conversion occurred over a number of years. He would come close to turning his life around and then fall back. Over time, the continued proximity to death and a restless heart forced him deeper into his relationship with Christ, and then his faith became inevitable and eventually took hold. The words to "Amazing Grace" were still many years off, but now he was no longer blind and could see.

Jesus's healing of the blind man symbolizes our own moment of seeing and giving in to a relationship with God. Like Newton, we fight back and sometimes must endure a great deal of hardship before we see. We struggle mightily at times to pursue this relationship with God. Sometimes we are in, and at other times we are out, but God persists through Jesus to bring our sight back. Then at some moment the events of our lives tip over our resistance and we, too, are no longer blind.

The backstory for John 9:25 reveals a person who was blind from birth that Jesus heals. The man is begging on the side of the road when Jesus sees him. The disciples ask Jesus if the beggar is blind because he was sinful or because his parents were sinful. Here Jesus begins his lesson.

Jesus and the disciples met the blind beggar on the Sabbath. To begin this lesson Jesus picks up mud and rubs it on the eyes of the blind man and tells him, **"Go, wash in the pool of Siloam."** (John 9:7) The man goes to the Siloam pool, which was just outside the city of Jerusalem (this pool was recently rediscovered in 2004 by workers in the underground plumbing systems of the city). After washing, the man can see, and he returns to his community, the members of which witness the change in him. They are, however, extraordinarily doubtful, wondering among themselves if this could be real, or if it were someone else they were meeting who looked like the blind man. Ironically, this same doubt occurs frequently even today with those who are spiritually reborn. Neighbors and friends, stuck in the past, wonder how the person could have been saved. They are not willing to completely accept the person's transformation.

After a long period of questioning, the people of his community ask the formerly blind man where Jesus is now, and the man answers, *"I do not know."* (John 9:12) The crowd brings the man to the Pharisees, who also doubt and ask numerous questions.

The Pharisees question the man's parents, who confirm that he was blind at birth. Not wanting to risk their status within the community, they avoid expressing any opinion about their son's healing and tell the Pharisees to talk to their son directly.

The Pharisees revisit the formerly blind man a second time and question him more aggressively. Trying to force him to acknowledge that it was God who healed him and not Jesus, they say, *"Give glory to God! We know this man is a sinner."* (John 9:24) The Pharisees were stuck on the fact that the healing was done on the Sabbath, a time when no one was supposed to work. They thus believed that Jesus had sinned by healing the man on the Sabbath. The Pharisees were more interested in discrediting Jesus than in understanding the healing. The man replies, *"I do not know whether he is a sinner. One thing I do know, that though I was blind, now I see."* (John 9:25)

Frustrated, the blind man further says, *"Here is an astonishing thing! You do not know where he comes from, and yet he opened my eyes. We know that God does not listen to sinners, but he does listen to one who worships him and obeys his will. Never since the world began has it been heard that anyone opened the eyes of a person born blind. If this man were not from God, he could do nothing."* (John 9:30–33)

Unwilling to accept this rebuke from the saved blind man, the Pharisees drive him out of his community. Imagine how we would feel if suddenly we were healed and then subjected to this kind of doubt and questioning. After a lifetime of blindness, this man no doubt imagined that those who surrounded him would be overjoyed at his sudden regaining of sight. Readers of this story can easily sympathize with the blind man and wonder why the Pharisees and his community could not come to terms with the fact that Jesus had healed him.

For those who were "blind" and now see, this is a common issue. Many will not believe that the miraculous change and healing

> *"One thing I do know, that though I was blind, now I see."*

came from an honorable cause. There must be some trick to it beyond just a change of heart or a healing. With Jesus that is all there is. As the blind beggar said so simply when asked how he was healed, *"I do not know whether he is a sinner. One thing I do know, that though I was blind, now I see."*

✝ ✝ ✝

Wrestling with God

I met John at a signing for my book *Jesus & Co*. He is the pastor of a small church in rural North Carolina. He would drift over to the table and look at my book and then wander away. After a few of these short visits, I sensed he wanted to say more, so I asked a few questions to draw out his story.

He told me about his current life as a pastor and believer, but he also revealed a deeper story. With his homespun drawl, John talked about the many nights when he had wrestled with God. He described it as a mighty fight. He had been prone to staying out late and drinking, which affected his work and his family. But he persisted in following this river in his life, despite its damaging effect. He knew it was wrong, but he did not feel he could change. He would try, only to slip back into what he perceived to be a place of comfort.

Then that moment came when he was stripped bare. He had lost his job and become completely alienated from his family. He had reached his tipping point, and his path had left him broken and alone. His comfortable habit of going out

> *"His comfortable habit of going out with the boys for long hours, which had affirmed his existence for years, had now left him nothing but desolation."*

with the boys for long hours, which had affirmed his existence for years, had now left him nothing but desolation.

Over the previous few months, he had been getting hints to change. Silently, he had begun to question on occasion if he was on the right path. His discourse with God had begun; however, there was still too much to let go of in his current life. He liked the familiar path, so he wrestled with God and resisted. Then it all came crashing down, and he was in a spot where he was so low he could only go up.

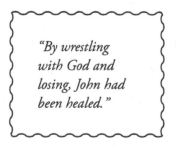

"By wrestling with God and losing, John had been healed."

At first, John began to read the Bible and, through this reading, to set his course to a different path. Over time, this extended to him getting an education and becoming a pastor. Both of which he accomplished.

John had a devoted wife and a life he was proud of and wanted to share. I saw, within both him and his wife, a faithful love for God. By wrestling with God and losing, John had been healed.

He had been blind but now he saw, and what he saw was a future that only contained a life filled with grace. He had been trapped, not because he was bad, but because he was following a path built on bad habits. A path that was familiar, even though it was destructive. He had given into his natural human tendencies to pursue this life in which he found satisfaction, even though it was only momentary. John wanted to do good, as most do, but he believed he would not find comfort anywhere else. In the Book of Romans, the apostle Paul says, *"I do not understand my own actions. For I do not do what I want, but I do the very thing I hate."* (Romans 7:15) Even the great apostle Paul struggled with this path and his own natural desires.

So it is always with our faith. It is a struggle to avoid doing what we should not do, to turn away from the wrong path and toward the right one. For some this may be easy, but for most, it is a hard lesson to learn, that many times the wrong path we choose only reveals its destructive nature in a valley of despair.

> "Faith is the consistent choosing of the narrow gate. Many times, following the narrow gate presents itself as a short-term loss, and its benefit is only revealed through a long-term lens."

Faith is the consistent choosing of the narrow gate. Many times, following the narrow gate presents itself as a short-term loss, and its benefit is only revealed through a long-term lens. A friend of mine who is a successful mountain climber talks about the painful first moments of ascending a steep mountain. To cope, he focuses only on the steps he is taking and avoids looking up or down. He just focuses on the moment at hand. When he reaches his climbing goal, he then looks back. He states, *"The joy I feel when I look back is always greater than the pain I endured."* In effect, the first steps are the hardest until he finds his rhythm, which leads to a satisfaction greater than the pain. John's journey to God was one step at a time.

✟ ✟ ✟

Looking at Ourselves as God Sees Us

People suffer not just from bad decision making but also from bad self-images. They feel they are not good enough, not even for God. They have been tricked in the past by viewing themselves in false comparisons to other people. Perhaps they have been told they are overweight or not pretty, or in some other way just do not measure up. This path of believing the negative things others say—or those we say to ourselves—is just as destructive as the lives of those who never question themselves at all but have taken the wrong path.

Sometimes we are our own worst enemies. When we believe what others say, we can become hard critics of ourselves and lose sight of the beauty of being made in God's image. In Genesis 1:27–28 it says, *"So God created humankind in his image, in the image of God he created them; male and female he created them."* When Jesus says, **"Follow me,"** some people do not assume Jesus means them, but he certainly does! They, too, are made in the image of God. Oftentimes a significant life event is required to muster up the strength to discover there is another path. A path of believing that we are worthy.

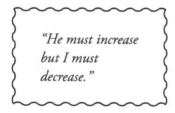

"He must increase but I must decrease."

This path to no longer being blind requires a giving up of ourselves. In the Gospel there is no better example of this than the story of John the Baptist. In John 3:30, John the Baptist says, *"He must increase but I must decrease."* A powerful statement from a man who was already recognized by his community as a major religious figure. At the time of this statement, John and Jesus had an overlapping ministry, but John was willing to give his up to not distract from Jesus's message of the "good news." He knew he was like the best man at a wedding and was more than willing to relinquish his own fame for that of the groom.

Those who are no longer blind have had to agree to the same submission. A walking away from themselves and toward walking with Jesus. Ironically, in this act of submission we become freed, no longer wedded to the world or what the world tells us.

✟　✟　✟

The Bible Helps Us See

A pastor friend of mine, Rich Teeters, relayed a story about a crusty police officer from Atlanta who was a member of his congregation. The man was forced by his wife to go to church and, reluctantly, each Sunday he went. At first, he sat and fidgeted. Then he started to like the music, but remained resistant. In the pulpit, Rich had noticed this man and became curious about him and his story. After service one Sunday he approached the man and asked him how he liked church. He replied, "I only come because my wife makes me come," then shrugged and walked away.

Over time, Rich continued to reach out to the police officer and engage in casual conversation after church. Later, Rich invited him to a history book club that the church held on Monday evenings. During this time, the police officer and Rich developed a closer friendship. Eventually Rich suggested, "Why don't you read the Bible each morning and see what happens?" Silently each morning, the police officer got up when the house was dark and began to read. Slowly at first. Then it became a habit. It became a part of his routine that he looked forward to each morning. With the rhythm of his morning Bible reading, he also began to pray. This combination of prayer and reading the Bible became a powerful elixir in his life. Over time his life took on more vibrancy, and the colors of the world he saw changed. They became brighter. Church started to mean something to him.

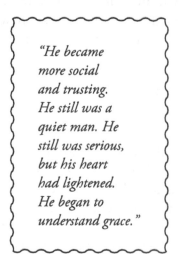

"He became more social and trusting. He still was a quiet man. He still was serious, but his heart had lightened. He began to understand grace."

Over the next year he read the whole Bible, a feat that he was proud of, something akin to running a marathon or riding a bike for a hundred miles. Rich also noticed some other things. He smiled more; he went to a Bible study class; and he began to participate in serving his community in other ways beyond being a police officer. Periodically, Rich would check in with his friend, and the man talked about a change of focus.

The man stated, *"I've become less interested in the news of the day and stopped obsessing about my savings account."* He became more social and trusting. He still was a quiet man. He still was serious, but his heart had lightened. He began to understand grace.

Today in America, a vast majority consider the Bible a sacred and blessed book, but only one in five read it even on a weekly basis. We might be too busy or stuck in our routines. We might be intimidated by its sacredness. The Bible is for us to read, to consider, and to be with in spirit. The Bible is the sacred Word of God. Critical to our faith development is believing that to be true. It is when we believe in the words of the Bible that we deepen our understanding of God and strengthen our faith in the unseen.

When we read the Bible on a routine basis, we will be affected. Slowly it will start to change us and cause us to think more about our actions and God. Over time, we will be more observant of God's presence around us and begin to see a different way to live.

The Bible removes our spiritual blindness and expands our existence from the limits of the world to the unlimited world of God. If we read the Bible for fifteen minutes a day, within a year we will have read it cover to cover. Perhaps like the police officer from Atlanta, we will see radical changes in our perspective on life. This daily reading means creating a new routine in our lives. Psychologists tell us that our routines become habit after doing the same thing for three weeks. These first weeks are the hardest However, when we have invited God's word into our hearts, the Bible becomes a companion and not just a book.

"If we read the Bible for fifteen minutes a day, within a year we will have read it cover to cover."

Jesus the Word came to reside among us and brought the Word of God. In the Bible we see the richness of his story. The Word was once among us and is still among us in the words of the Bible. What stands before us is grace and truth.

We have all been blind, but we all yearn to see. We wrestle with God in our minds and in our lives to gain our vision. As time moves on, we begin to veer onto the path of spiritual sight. Pushed by a compelling force, our prayers, and the Bible. Investing this time in our faith heals us.

CHAPTER 5

FREELY YOU HAVE RECEIVED; FREELY GIVE

"'The kingdom of heaven has come near. Heal the sick, raise the dead, cleanse those who have leprosy, drive out demons. Freely you have received; freely give."

—Matthew 10:7–8

Give Freely

After Jesus had assembled and trained the band of twelve apostles, he sat them down to give them instructions on how to help him with his earthly mission. Instructions for them to proceed forward and heal the sick, raise the dead, cleanse those with leprosy, and drive out demons. By now they had seen Jesus do these wonderful things throughout the Judean world. Now it was their turn to move forward with their faith in Jesus and become world changers.

Jesus tells them, *"Freely you have received; freely give."* A command to be generous and open within their newfound faith. Jesus wants them to walk among the people and help them with their daily lives, not in judgment, but with generosity.

They had been given the mighty gift of faith, and it was now their turn to give.

So it is with us. Jesus wants us to have an empathetic heart filled with generosity. A heart that does not judge, but desires to give. A heart that knows even the smallest gift or kindness can change a life. To have a desire that first considers others' plight and then is moved to help. There are many in the world that need our help, and we should give freely. In this giving we are both redeemed and redeeming.

✟ ✟ ✟

The Thankful Leper

Jesus shows this attitude of generosity in helping while visiting a colony of lepers. Jesus is walking on the border between Galilee and Samaria and comes across an outpost that holds a leper colony. He enters this village of castoffs and hears from ten men, *"Jesus, Master, have mercy on us!"* (Luke 17:13) These ten men have been forced to live away from their families and friends.

Because of the devastatingly contagious nature of leprosy and the lack of modern medical treatment in the first century, people who contracted this disease had to leave their homes and community. Also, from a precautionary standpoint during that time, a person with *any* skin ailment would be considered a leper. Fear of contracting leprosy was a paramount concern in the first century.

Ironically, this leper outpost was on the border that separated two very different worlds. For the most part, Galilee was populated by the remnants of Judah, one of twelve tribes that had settled in Judea. And Samaria was the area inhabited by those from the other twelve tribes, which had separated from Judah after the death of King Solomon many centuries earlier.

These two communities, separately, represented the original twelve tribes of Israel that had inherited the promised land. A separation born out of splintered leadership and human disagreements.

Therefore, a large gulf existed between these two communities. However, in the leper colony, both remnants of the original twelve tribes existed side by side, connected by a terrible disease.

The belief in Palestine at that time was that leprosy was caused by God, and the leper was considered unclean both physically and spiritually. The disease itself is horrifying, with boils, disfigurement, and nerve pain being common symptoms. Most people would be separated from their families for the balance of their lives. Today, the bacteria that causes leprosy is easily treated and has become rare in the developed world. In the United States only around one hundred cases occur each year.

In the first century, however, these people knew they were doomed to live a life apart from others—never to hold their children or eat with their families again. They knew they would suffer for long periods, as the disease was chronic. The plea of these ten men to Jesus was one of abject desperation.

Jesus takes pity on them and cleanses them. In addition, he tells them, *"Go and show yourselves to the priests."* (Luke 17:14) It was a practical command, so that they could become reunited with their own communities by receiving the priest's acknowledgment they were now healed.

One of the men from Samaria went back, praising God and falling at Jesus's feet. Knowing the gift he had been given, he was overwhelmed with gratitude for having being released from a life of isolation caused by a terrible disease.

Seeing this, Jesus asks, *"Were not ten made clean? But the other nine, where are they? Was none of them found to*

return and give praise to God except this foreigner?" Then
Jesus said to the thankful leper, *"Get up and go on your way;
your faith has made you well."* (Luke 17:17–19)

We can wonder about the other nine, but the deeper story
of faith lies with the one who returned—a remarkable contrast
to the nine. We notice that Jesus says to him, *"your faith has
made you well."* For the others, the healing was a miracle,
but for the lone person who returned to Jesus, his faith in
God effected a more profound cure. He was once a desperate
person, who'd certainly prayed to be healed, and through Jesus
his prayer was answered. Moreover, his return to give thanks
and his recognition of how he was healed shows us that he
would long remember how it happened.

During his time of trouble and isolation, it would have
been easy to say to the leper, *"Get up and dust yourself off."* Many
of us have heard this encouragement, but it is not so easy to do.
Perhaps we have had a major financial setback or are struggling with a relationship. In those silent moments by ourselves,
we twist, and we turn, searching for answers. We head down
various mental paths and look in each corner. Perhaps we cry
out or silently yell that it's not fair, and it probably isn't. It is
true that we should just get up, dust ourselves off, and go on,
but it is not that easy for everyone.

For the leper, life had been hard, but he pressed on in his
search and called out to Jesus. In the moment of his darkest
night, he was healed, not just by Jesus, but also by his faith in
Jesus. He now becomes a person who was healed in a moment.
In his thankfulness, we can see a committed heart that will be
generous.

Jesus provides us with grace and a newness in our lives. He
gives us a heightened sense of empathy for our neighbor and
redirects how we look at life. Scarcity and want ebb in this new
life. Peace is found through the desire for the rewards of heaven

> *"Jesus provides us with grace and a newness in our lives."*

and not of the world. The leper was not only cleansed, but his faith made him well at a deeper level, for which he showed thankfulness and the acknowledgment of where the healing came from: his faith and Jesus.

This faith will also generate a generosity that is real. A giving back to help others out of our own bounty. Generosity is one of the fruits of our faith. An indication that our faith and healing are real.

✟　✟　✟

Living a Life of Thankfulness

Jesus knows we worry about not having enough. He knows our temptation to want more at any cost. With his grace we do receive a life of bounty—not always a material bounty but always a spiritual one. Our faith opens our eyes to this bounty and implores us to share what we have received. Not to be hemmed in by the temptations of the world to retain our bounty, but to share. When we have a generous heart, we in turn become healed from the worry of scarcity, no longer burdened by the thought, *Will I have enough?*

I have a friend named Linda who describes the joy of giving as a byproduct of generosity. She gives every day, not to receive, but because she is moved by the needs of others. The great joy she receives is through helping. In her community there is a pocket of poverty so severe that children do not have coats to wear in the winter. These children's last meal of the day may be lunch at school. High schoolers will not have enough money to buy clothes for their prom. It is into this world that Linda enters.

Recently, the school social worker approached her and told her about a young man who did not have the sneakers he needed for his training in the Reserve Officers' Training Corps (ROTC). The officer of the local ROTC had called the school to see if there was a way to get him some. Immediately upon hearing this, Linda went to the local Walmart and bought a pair of sneakers, and as she always does, she bought a little more. She bought the young man three pairs of socks.

Upon delivery of these gifts to the school's social worker, the boy was called into the office. The social worker explained that these new sneakers were his to wear to his ROTC training.

When the boy saw the sneakers, he was stunned. He said, *"These can't be mine. I never get new sneakers, and these are too nice for me."*

The social worker replied, *"They are yours, and you have earned them."*

Seeing socks tucked into the sneakers, the boy asked, *"Whose socks are these in the sneakers?"*

"They are yours as well!"

"I can't accept them," the boy said. *"Please give them to someone else with greater needs. I have socks already."*

It is for these moments Linda gives. Her heart pounds with joy. This delightfully charming woman lives not to receive but to give. To give because she should.

While Linda will tell you that she is now blessed with a wonderful husband who adores her and neighbors who give her great joy, there is a backstory to her life. A life of challenges and hurdles. A life where her consistent and unwavering faith steadied her and kept her personal ship afloat.

Linda was promised college but could only attend for one year. The effort to drive hours to school each week, study, and then work to pay her bills was too large of a requirement.

Needing money to live, Linda entered the full-time workforce as a bank teller.

She said to herself, *If this is what I now must do, I will be the best and learn all I can.* At eighteen she started her new life, with a riveted focus on being the best. As is typical with Linda, she learned every job and became the best bank employee she could be. Her bank made her a trainer, and she would train male branch managers, then watch them get good jobs she herself was more than qualified to handle. This was in the 1960s, and the workplace was extraordinarily unfair to qualified women. Although Linda knew this, she continued to do an extraordinary job training these men because she felt she should.

After a few years, she married. Her first husband asked her to change churches, which she did. However, she soon noticed flaws in her first husband. On the outside, he was all that a Christian should be, but privately he did not live those values. Linda stayed strong and continued to be a good wife and a mother to her two children. Over time her husband's behavior produced crisis after crisis in Linda's life. She gave up, but her life began to change.

At work, she finally got promoted to a job that should have been hers many years earlier. Her employer had been left this time with few choices, and new leadership recognized this steadfast and loyal woman by giving her the job she deserved.

Later, she left banking and went on to become a highly successful salesperson. Consistent with her early life, she worked hard, and each month for thirteen years, she was either the number one or number two salesperson at her company. During this time, she also met her second husband. A man who blessed her not only with support but also with the adoration she had always deserved. She had been cleansed from a punishing life she had not deserved.

"Linda gives because she has received."

Today, Linda gives. It is her life. She helps her neighbors. In fact, each New Year's Day she bakes for her neighbors and joyously invites them to her house. They pile into her place and enjoy the gifts of a caring and giving woman. She has amassed a large number of gowns for the kids in her area so they can go to the prom looking like a million dollars. Each year she provides new shoes to children who do not have them for school. They all know this giving woman cares. She helps many children born into poverty—not because she is looking for credit, but because they deserve it, and she believes she should help them. Linda gives because she has received. In her giving she heals and is healed.

✟ ✟ ✟

Living to Please Him in Every Way

Henry Parsons Crowell was the President of Quaker Oats. He lost a lot in the early part of his life. His father died at thirty-six of tuberculosis. He himself nearly died from the same disease. He could not get a high school diploma because he had to work to help his family after his father's death. His first wife died after two and a half years. The first part of his life was hard.

By 1885, he had started to have some success in business and bought a company called Quaker Oats. He made one small change to the company. Instead of selling his cereal in large barrels, he introduced the smaller containers we are familiar with today, making the cereal more available to consumers. Soon, Quaker Oats became available in grocery stores throughout the country. During the depression of 1893, it served as a cost-saving staple for many American families.

Soon after, Henry remarried and began to use his faith-life to help others. He introduced God into the business world and to other tycoons, such as John Rockefeller. Henry and his wife travelled the country, contributing to many organizations. In some years he would donate to one hundred organizations. He is famously quoted as saying, *"If my life can be lived so as to please Him in every way, I'll be supremely happy."* In the last years of his life, Henry was constantly working for the Lord.

> *"If my life can be lived so as to please Him in every way, I'll be supremely happy."*

Jesus famously said, **"My Father is still working, and I also am working."** (John 5:17) The backstory to the verse is that Jesus had just healed a person on the Sabbath. The religious elite complained mightily and tried to use this against Jesus. Jesus's reply to those of the first century speaks directly to our Christian behavior in the twenty-first century. He extends our work for God to include Sunday. We have our work lives that we use to pay our bills. From that, we should have a Sabbath. We also have the work of the Lord, which never ceases. Every action, twenty-four hours a day, seven days a week, that helps God, and humankind is in

> *"Every action, twenty-four hours a day, seven days a week, that helps God and humankind is in concert with God."*

concert with God. We need our rest, and we should take it, but we should not be wedded to legalism but rather to the Spirit of God.

Henry Crowell died in 1948. He left a large trust. In his will he left his trustees with a clear directive: *"To carry out Mr. Crowell's wishes to honor the Lord who he loved and served during his life on this earth."* Over the years the trustees have kept this wish alive. Each year they issue close to 150 grants, totaling millions of dollars. Well past his death, Henry Crowell is still working for the Lord. He was dubbed the "Cereal Tycoon" and created a life of riches with one small change to his business, and he also created a life that worked endlessly for *"the Lord who he loved."*

Both Linda and Henry gave because they felt blessed and in turn shared their blessings. They had a heart for God and for the needy.

✟   ✟   ✟

The Deeper Story Behind Why We Give

A friend of mine, Tom Locke, runs an extraordinarily successful organization called the Texas Methodist Foundation, based in Austin, Texas. Tom is a premier networker and is very open about his faith. It is not uncommon to get a call from Tom where his only objective is to stay connected—an unusual trait in our busy world. Tom starts every conversation with, *"How are you doing?"* It's a sincere question with a desired interest in hearing your answer. Gracious and giving in all that he does, Tom is an advocate for God. In the meals I have had with Tom, he asks that we pray. When Tom makes this request, it lifts my spirits and heartens my soul. Also, Tom frequently expresses his gratitude to God for the wonderful life he has been given. He is an earnest man with a sense of responsibility to his work that those of us who know him greatly admire. He leads a blessed life, with a wonderful wife, children, and grandchildren.

Tom has run the Texas Methodist Foundation for decades. Over that period, it has grown from having a few million dollars in assets to close to a billion. It lends money to churches, helps the poor, and provides leadership training for the church. Tom has been able to blend his faithful life with great business acumen. He will quickly tell you that it is not because of him that his organization has thrived; it is because of the many people who work with him. It is true that Tom has surrounded himself with extraordinary people; however, he has also created an environment where they can excel and express their own faithful desires. Tom attracts good people because he gives.

"When was the first time you gave in your life?"

One of Tom's jobs is fundraising to support the many philanthropic programs of the Texas Methodist Foundation. His approach to this effort is highly unusual. First, he asks one question to everyone he meets: *"When was the first time you gave in your life?"* This demonstrates his sincere interest in knowing the story and also a desire to learn more about the individual.

In these answers, he finds very deep and personal stories about faithful Christians. He finds a depth of gratitude that will bring many to tears when they tell Tom why they first gave. A cleansing that occurs as people reflect on all they have received. He discovers that they give because they have received from God. To most, it is an overwhelming response of gratitude at both knowing God exists and a very intense appreciation for what they have been given.

Tom does not ask this question to stir up the emotion that lies beneath the surface, but he is always amazed at its intensity.

Many of these conversations become a therapeutic response to his simple question. When Tom and I talk about why this happens, we are both struck by the strong current of emotion that exists when people are in a safe environment to discuss their faith. I saw this same emotion in many of my interviews for this book. A drawing out of the gratitude that simmers beneath the exterior of all who believe.

As I reflected on therapeutic responses Tom received, I went back to Genesis 1:27, where it states, *"So God created human-kind in his image, in the image of God he created them; male and female he created them."* As we are made in the image of God, one of the wonderful attributes acquired is that of generosity. A desire to give and to help, injected in each of us from birth. When we give, we act in the Spirit of God. We live into our image of God, and whenever we give, we satisfy this spirit of generosity. We are left with a joy that is directly connected to our birthright of being made in the image of God. Tom's question draws this sense of joy to the surface and invokes strong emotions that are directly connected to our desire to have a God-like sense of compassion. We are, in this moment, connected to God.

Tom continues to work as hard today as he did yesterday. Each day, Tom is driven by his sense of responsibility to his organization's wonderful mission of serving God and his desire to help. Tom has many friends who trust him because he cares first and asks second. He inspires us because he gives each of us space to be creative and express ourselves. In addition, Tom provides a beacon of responsibility to our Lord that inspires each of us to give freely.

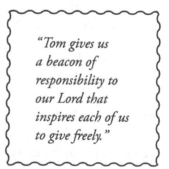

"Tom gives us a beacon of responsibility to our Lord that inspires each of us to give freely."

✝ ✝ ✝

Whom Do We Serve?

The spirit of generosity comes from a faith that heals. This promotes a different perspective on life—a place where we begin to separate that which is important and that which is not. Jesus explains this by saying, *"No slave can serve two masters; for a slave will either hate the one and love the other or be devoted to the one and despise the other. You cannot serve God and wealth."* (Luke 16:13) When we are healed by our faith, we can see this difference; material wants disappear and are replaced with spiritual desires. No longer does the BMW matter, but living in peace with God does. Peer pressure is replaced by the desire to be good and be generous. We no longer need to be the first off at the green light. We are now willing to wait for someone else to be first in line. Giving replaces getting.

John Tyson, CEO of Tyson Foods, has hired more than one hundred chaplains for his workforce. The chaplains deal with family matters, drug and alcohol addiction, and faith issues. Tyson's company freely invests in its main asset—its employees—by giving back to those who produce tangible results for the corporation. In turn, the employees regularly serve meals to those affected by disaster under a program called "Meals That Matter." The company has won the International Spirit at Work Award. Not all the employees are Christian, but all are accepted and give.

When John was younger, he dealt with his own demons. He suffered from alcoholism and ventured far off the path. John had traveled a different road from most—a road built by privilege. He had all he needed materially, but he used wealth for himself and not others. Eventually, the alcohol created a life crisis. It was here, as an alcoholic, that he began to turn to a road of faith and giving, and through his faith he recovered. John changed his perspective from being served to serving.

However, when his father was set to turn the company over to John, the board of directors had very serious concerns because of John's past. Through several conversations, John was able to assure them of his worthiness by convincing them that he would serve and not be served. What persuaded the board to promote John was his deep faith. He was made CEO, and in 2000 he implemented the chaplain program at Tyson Foods.

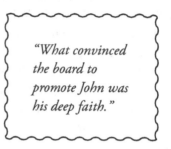

"What convinced the board to promote John was his deep faith."

The verse about serving two masters, Luke 16:13, is from the Parable of the Dishonest Manager. In this parable Jesus points out the pitfalls of self-interest and of not serving God and your neighbor first. It is a parable not about whether being rich is good or bad but about whom we serve. When we work, do we keep Jesus's tenet of "love your God and love your neighbor" foremost? Or do we dive deeper into our own ambitions and wants? When we work, do we think about how it can benefit others? Do we think about fair play with our employees and other employees? "Where are our hearts, and whom do we serve?" is the critical question.

The temptation to serve ourselves and money is persistent. It has the potential to control our every action each day, hour, and minute. Following the path of materialism will

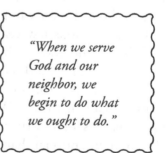

"When we serve God and our neighbor, we begin to do what we ought to do."

change the truths we tell ourselves. We are constantly beset with the choice of serving money or something greater. Serving money and ourselves may have significant short-term gains but will usually end poorly. When we serve God and our neighbor, we begin to do what we ought to do, and what will benefit us most in the long run.

The decisions we make are always choices between serving ourselves or serving generously. Jesus is clear we cannot serve both. When we decide our path, we can decide on wealth, power, and worldly approval, or we can decide on God and our neighbor.

✟   ✟   ✟

Giving of Ourselves

I had seen him earlier in the afternoon, hovering close to my book outpost. I was conducting a book signing in a small town in North Carolina, and since I am a relatively unknown writer, over the course of a few hours not many came. However, I do love doing them because I get to see and meet real humanity. People who have stories that inspire and teach me. Near the end of the day, he finally came forward and introduced himself. Mark was at one time married, but he had lost his wife because of an affair she had. He had once been a traffic reporter, but now he was a part-timer, a filmmaker. Now he was lonely; however, he had a story to tell.

In the previous few years, he had moved to a trailer on a pond. The pond was the habitat of twenty-five ducks, which got free food and health care through Mark. Long before, he had dropped his dreams of riches and instead turned to a life without material things. When he writes to his friends and family, he uses a typewriter and not a computer, feeling that it is far more intentional than a hastily crafted email.

Our conversation was very one-sided; he went from one story to another. This lonely man had found an audience in me and had an incredibly urgent desire to tell me everything. As I listened, I prayed for guidance. *Do I continue to sit and just listen, or do I cut him short?* A wave of empathy swept over me, and I settled back and listened for half an hour as this earnest, faithful, and kind man revealed his life story.

Finally, it was five o'clock, the book signing was over, and I had to go. We exchanged cards, and I will reach out to him again, even though he will likely be the only one talking. By listening, I was giving validation to a lonely man. A good man with an earnest and faithful heart. Too old now to change his future and spurned by a society that considers age a disability. I gave, but I also received. I learned what was important. It was not about how many books I sold but the uncovering of a wonderful person who understood life.

It is not just about giving up our material possessions. The lesson for me that day was that I could also give the gift of time, which for some is all they have to give. For that small sacrifice on my part, I received a spiritual gift in return.

In the Sermon on the Mount, Jesus's first sermon, he says, ***"In the same way, let your light shine before others, so that they may see your good works and give glory to your Father in heaven."*** (Matthew 5:16) Light is often associated with Jesus. In fact, in the four Gospels the word is used thirty-nine times. Jesus implores us to remember that our light can uplift. A smile can change a day. Our good work, likewise, should not be hidden. Delivered with the light of our hearts and Jesus, it becomes a beacon.

We give because we have received. We continue to give because we are made in the image of God. Our works are shown because we have faith. In this faith we are healed, and we heal when we give. Our faith shows before others as a bright light.

CHAPTER 6

ANOINTING THE BROKEN

"And he said to the woman, 'Your faith has saved you;
go in peace.'"

—LUKE 7:50

Saved from a Difficult Life

Jesus is invited by Simon, a well-known Pharisee, to his house for dinner. Soon after Jesus arrives, a woman of questionable repute also arrives at Simon's house. She had heard Jesus was going to be there, and because of her low social status, she had a limited opportunity to meet with Jesus. This was her chance to be redeemed. She'd had a difficult life; some of her bad luck was her fault, and some, the circumstances of life. She desperately wanted to change the course of her life. A compelling feeling inside of her knew Jesus was the answer. She only had to barge into Simon's house and move quickly.

She arrived at Simon's house with a jar of expensive ointment and quickly walked over to Jesus. Standing behind him, she begins to weep—hard enough to wet Jesus's feet, which she then dries with her hair. As she does so, she begins kissing his feet and applies ointment. She is in front of God, crying and in complete submission. Completely and fully, she bares her soul.

In the first century, the washing of feet was far more important than it is today. The roads were dusty, and most walked wearing only sandals. Feet soiled very quickly, and the washing of feet was of paramount importance. Few acts of kindness were greater than washing and anointing another person's feet.

Seeing all of this, Simon the Pharisee, thinks to himself, *If this man were a prophet, he would have known who and what kind of woman this is who is touching him—that she is a sinner.* Jesus, knowing what he is thinking, asks the man, **"A certain creditor had two debtors, one owed five hundred denarii, and the other owes fifty denarii. When they could not pay, he canceled the debts for both of them. Now which of them will love him more?"**

Simon replies, *"I suppose the one for whom he canceled the greater debt."*

Jesus says, **"You have judged rightly. Do you see this woman? I entered your house; you gave me no water for my feet, but she bathed my feet with her tears and dried them with her hair. You gave me no kiss, but from the time I came in she has not stopped kissing my feet. You did not anoint my head with oil, but she has anointed my feet with ointment."**

Jesus goes on to say, **"Her sins, which were many, have been forgiven; hence she has shown great love. But the one to whom little is forgiven, loves little."**

Jesus then calls the woman over and tells her, **"Your sins are forgiven."** This surprises the other dinner guests, who remark, *"Who is this who even forgives sin?"*

Ignoring this comment, Jesus looks back at the woman and says, **"Your faith has saved you; go in peace."** (Luke 7:41–50) Her brokenness healed, she now knew that, despite her lowly and difficult life, God loved her. The deep yearning to receive

God's acceptance and change her life had been answered. This yearning to see God and be with God created a flood of emotion that rose to the surface and expressed itself through tears and adoration. Her faith in Jesus had healed her.

✝ ✝ ✝

Even the Homeless are Worthy to Sit in a Chapel

As part of my education, I had to serve a church as an intern. My assignment was to help two other students revive a very broken church in a poor area along the Jersey Shore. The church had declined from three hundred attending members to only ten or so every Sunday morning. As in many churches today, the message was no longer resonating with the congregation. Specifically, for this church, the influx of poverty had caused most of the members to turn away. This church also had the added issue of a changing demographic. What had once been an affluent community had, over time, become inhabited by homeless people and others with meager means.

The previous pastor had tried to introduce a ministry to help the poor and homeless and received little support from the congregation. Over time, she created a feeding and clothing program, but she was transferred to another church. The three of us were left to pick up her work and help the congregation move forward.

We continued to run the feeding and clothing program, thanks in large part to a young and extraordinarily bright and wise intern, Lakesha Groover. Lakesha welcomed all with open arms and slowly over time won the hearts of homeless people. Lakesha and Andrew, the other intern, suggested we start a Sunday breakfast program in the dining hall for the homeless, with the hopes of then having them attend church afterward. My assignment was to get up each Sunday at five in the morning and ask local merchants to provide the food. I visited many of the restaurants and knew the ones who displayed a Christian message, like a cross, would help.

We would set up and be ready for breakfast by eight. We also recruited a friend who made blueberry cobbler each Saturday night. Jim Whitehead would show up with his cobbler and usually some sausage for the people. Many Sundays, fifty or so people would arrive.

After a few weeks, we started to hold church in the dining area to make it easier for those attending to stay. The ten or so existing members were also asked to join in. All refused, making comments like, "This is ridiculous; this isn't church," or "You have ruined our church." And so it went.

Interestingly, prior to this point, the church had run out of funds and did not have enough money to pay its utility bills. The church was essentially bankrupt. Despite our efforts to try another way to revive their church, the existing congregation wanted to stay rooted in a bankrupt church that could no longer pay its bills.

We were able to secure funding through the generous help of Bishop John Schol of the United Methodist Church and personal funds from myself. Enough to keep us afloat for another six months. We continued trying to revive the church by focusing on those in need.

Soon the homeless asked why they could not sit in the chapel. We said, *"Of course you can."* We were delighted that they wanted to be together in the chapel. What was interesting about this group was the way they sang their favorite hymns, with gusto; and their prayers were for simple things, like food, clothing, and shelter. Whenever I gave a sermon, I was always interrupted. People would stop me and tell me they had a different interpretation or that my comments reminded them of an event. In effect, each of my sermons became a guided dialogue and a debate. A debate that showed me the depth of their desire to know God.

We started to get to know the people and their individual journeys. Most were alcoholics or addicts, often driven to self-medicate due to an underlying mental illness caused by some previous trauma in their life. Many came from broken homes, where their start in life had been far more diminished than most. Many had served time in prison and could not find a job because they had a record. Occasionally, there would be an outburst we had to subdue, but mostly there was joy for us and those attending.

As time wore on and our stint was drawing to an end, a new supervisor arrived who was not supportive of a church that could not pay for itself. Despite our protests, we had no luck changing minds.

However, the church did have a viable option to save itself financially. I pointed out that the church property was worth somewhat more than a million dollars—enough to invest and use the proceeds to rent space and continue the work. But administrators outside of the church invoked too much red tape, and the church was doomed because of a document written long ago that prevented the church from being sold. Instead, the church continued to be cash poor but real estate rich.

Near the end of my stay, we held a Christmas Eve service, which was well attended. We sang, ate, and learned. I had discovered that these people were heroes. Sure, I had to tell them no swearing, no smoking on church grounds, and, especially, no weapons in church! They loved Jesus and wanted to be loved by Jesus. They showed

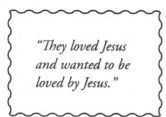

"They loved Jesus and wanted to be loved by Jesus."

up in a place they were not normally invited and, for a brief period, they were whole as Christians. For those short few months, they had a church and a place to eat.

Perhaps we were too idealistic or maybe unrealistic, but as a group, we never understood why their lives had to be so different from our own. They were one step away from normalcy, and only because of the self-destructive effect of addiction. Their addictions were so strong they prevented them from being part of a normal family structure. They self-medicated their pain, but these were still people even though they were homeless and shunned by their neighbors and society. For a brief period, they were being healed as a community.

Jesus says the sins of the broken are forgiven through their faith. Can we forgive?

✞ ✞ ✞

Grandmothers That Guide Us in Our Faith

My friend Jonelle is a woman whose faith is so near her surface that she tears up when she discusses it. It is a joyous and thankful moment for her. Her distant past was far less joyous than her present life. She is a woman who, early on, was not given many flat and straight roads. But she is also a woman who used this early life to build an internal faith that seeps out in every conversation she has about it.

Jonelle's parents got divorced when she was very young. Her mother left the house and had little contact with Jonelle after that. Her dad moved her a lot, and she had a number of stepmoms. She remembers none of them well, except for one particularly difficult one. As she became a young adult, even though Jonelle's weight was in proportion to her height, she was called "fat" by her family, who followed the lead of this one difficult stepmother. Her younger sister was smaller, and she received all the praise. Without structure and with a significant amount of chaos around her, Jonelle joined the Marines after high school—a move that would provide her with structure and a caring community for the first time.

In the Marines she began to stabilize. Later, she would marry and have two children. However, the marriage ended in divorce, and she was forced to raise her children as a single mom. She pressed on again.

Fortunately, she met her second husband, and her life began to stabilize once more. She finally had a consistent and caring life partner. Someone she could count on. A partner who fully embraced her and her children. She finally had firm ground.

Today Jonelle is successful in her career. She and her husband have started their own business, which is beginning to generate extra cash. Life is good for her now.

In interviewing her for this book, I asked her several questions about her strong faith development. I was curious about where it had come from, despite her early life chaos. Her reply was that her faith had come from her grandmother, the only stable force in her early life. Her grandmother taught her that it was okay to pray and ask God for help, and she stayed close to Jonelle during the difficult years of frequent moves and new stepmoms.

Her grandmother died five months before Jonelle remarried, but Jonelle has always felt her grandmother's spirit near her, even when her grandmother was far away. That did not change after her death. Her grandmother loved her and cared for her, similar to how

> "Her grandmother loved her and cared for her, similar to how Jonelle views her personal relationship with Jesus."

Jonelle views her personal relationship with Jesus. To this day, she still feels the presence of her grandmother in both the good and dark times of her life. A spiritual presence that still brings her faith very close to the surface. She knows it was the combination of her grandmother and Jesus that brought her to a life of stability.

As Jonelle mentioned her grandmother during my interview, I immediately went to memories of my own grandmother. Unlike Jonelle, I had a very strong and supportive set of parents, but my grandmother Eleanor has been and is a strong spiritual force in my life.

My grandmother was a hardworking woman who, like Jonelle, absorbed a lot in life. An alcoholic husband forced her to work extremely hard to keep her family together. She was a highly regarded nurse who excelled in her profession despite an unstable home life. Any visit by her grandchildren was always met with warmth and hugs. We all loved her. She died when I was fifteen.

Through I've had mostly a good life, I've always felt her spiritually close, even after her death when I was a teenager. In both the high points and low spots, she was always there. Thoughts of her always bring strong emotions of joy and thankfulness. The mere mention of her today will bring on a wave of deep emotion for me. Other than Jesus, her spirit is the only force I turn to in need. Like Jonelle, my grandmother's spirit is a place of comfort.

Over the years Jonelle has dealt with forgiveness. Learning to let go of her hidden anger toward a very difficult step-mother and dad. A belief that if she is to be forgiven, then she must forgive. As time has worn

> *"A belief that if she is to be forgiven, then she must forgive."*

on, it has become easier to forgive. In part because she prays daily and sees her prayers answered. In part because she has a good life now, with a stable home and the bounty of belonging.

She has become a wonderful, God fearing woman. A person who was broken but is now made well, with a steady and forthright approach to life. Her faith is always evident in our conversations. She loves Jesus and is unashamed of this love. The emotions that rise to the surface when she discusses her faith are those of joy and thankfulness.

✟ ✟ ✟

Even the Mighty Will Become Trapped

In 1978, Betty Ford's family confronted her about her alcoholism and addiction to opiates. In her memoirs she later stated, *"I liked alcohol, it made me feel warm. And I loved pills. They took away my tension and pain."* Here was a former First Lady admitting her addiction. A former First Lady who was well regarded for her social activism and grace. Despite her power and status, she had been trapped.

After her family's intervention, she entered rehab and emerged into recovery. Behind her life as a social activist, a breast cancer survivor, and an abused wife in her first marriage, was a hidden life of booze and drugs. The pressures of her past and present had driven her into the trap.

Later, she set up the famous Betty Ford Center. In its time, it became the go-to place for addiction recovery. Betty Ford's public admission of her situation has helped over one hundred thousand people take the first steps to recovery, but Betty Ford was more than this. She also inspired women struggling with breast cancer. She fought for women's rights by lobbying for passage of the Equal Rights Amendment. In 1991, she was awarded the Presidential Medal of Freedom.

Near the end of Jesus's mission on earth, he issues a warning, saying, **"Be on guard so that your hearts are not weighed down with dissipation and drunkenness and the worries of this life, and that day does not catch you unexpectedly, like a trap. For it will come upon all who live on the face of the whole earth."** (Luke 21:34–35)

> *"Jesus tells us that all will be confronted. None will escape the battle. Not even First Ladies of great character."*

In this verse, Jesus tells us to be on guard against life's addictions of all kinds. He calls them a trap that arises unexpectedly. Jesus also tells us that all will be confronted. None will escape the battle. Not even First Ladies of great character. It can become an embarrassing moment in our lives that we try to conceal. In this concealment, we lose the resources of friends who can help. We may also conceal our addiction and silent lives from God, who *will* help. We fight alone against a dangerous foe. Our embarrassment prevents resources from coming to our aid. We become trapped. It is inevitable that we all encounter this part of life in one form or another. Our faith development will be challenged, and we will have to fight back mightily to retain our faith and ourselves.

How do we win against addiction and life's traps? Jesus says through prayer and our faith. We should pray for strength to escape these things, but it starts with admitting that we are being confronted. We need to extend this recognition into prayer. We need to allow others in on the secret, as Betty Ford was forced to do. Our faith, prayers, friends, and, most importantly, our recognition of our addictions become our shield. There will be those who judge, but they will have their turn. They, too, will need help in the future. We press forward, balancing judgment against recovery. Assisting those in recovery is far stronger; judgment, far weaker.

Even one of our country's most gracious First Ladies became entrapped. Sinking into the abyss of brokenness, she found herself alone, hiding her addiction. Through her faith, prayers, family, and friends she recovered. And not only did she recover, she turned her personal tragedy into a beacon of hope for others.

We all will enter this moment in our lives. Hopefully, it is a temporary test of our faith. When we emerge into recovery, we can renew our lives and begin the task of being a shining light for others. We become healed.

✝ ✝ ✝

The Road Behind Us Is Not Where We Are Going

One of the hardest things in emerging from recovery or brokenness is forgiving ourselves and leaving our past behind. In 2 Corinthians 5:17, the apostle Paul reminds us of the new creation we have become by saying, *"So if anyone is in Christ, there is a new creation; everything old has passed away; see, everything has become new!"* A promise for those who are broken that life can become new again.

> *"Exposed by sin as an impostor, he began the process of reevaluating his life and taking the long road back."*

A client of mine had a very personal self-inflicted catastrophe. After living a life that was driven to pursue power, money, and fame, he took a step too far. As he achieved more and more, he began to cut corners in all aspects of his life. He began to see his friends and family as a way to get what he wanted and to ignore their human value. He had become trapped in the lure of power and took the fateful step that went too far. Exposed by sin as an impostor, he began the process of reevaluating his life and taking the long road back. He turned to Jesus and accepted the yoke of being born again.

He changed his priorities. He began to work to provide for his family and not for himself. He reentered the church and became a person of service. He relearned the values of "loving your neighbor." He came home for dinner to be with his family and avoided late-night meetings. With these changes, he received forgiveness from those close to him. Though the climb back was hard and uneven, he persisted and stayed riveted on the values of Jesus. Still, in our counseling sessions, I noticed he had one hard step left to climb—he had to forgive himself.

In the verse attributed to the apostle Paul at the beginning of this section, we see the term "new creation." Paul tells us that when we fully turn to a life with Jesus, we become a new person or being. Our priorities change, and we change with them. Life is new. It is not that we do not have to pay for the consequences of our past, but that the past no longer defines who we are. When we reconcile with God and our neighbor, we are forgiven. However, the hardest person to forgive for our past is ourselves. We often drift back and fall into despair when we think about our past. We question who we are and become embarrassed at what we have done. We cannot release ourselves from our guilt.

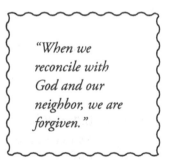

"When we reconcile with God and our neighbor, we are forgiven."

My client's toughest critic was himself. He tried to over-achieve in his new life to escape his past. Every error in judgment brought on harsh self-criticism. He could not forgive himself as he tried to outrun his past. He over-helped and over-apologized. He had not released himself, despite the renewed acceptance from friends, family, and Jesus. He could not move away from the regret of his past, so his recovery was incomplete. Each journey he took to review his past brought horror and self-loathing.

> "He now understood that it is not where we have been but where we are going on the road in front of us that is important."

Eventually, he believed the words of Paul and moved forward. Eventually, he accepted the love of his family, friends, and Jesus. Eventually, he stopped judging himself based on the past and looked to the present. He now understood that it is not where we have been but where we are going on the road in front of us that is important. It is in the present, as a new creation with the Lord, that Jesus wants us to walk.

✟ ✟ ✟

Cheering for the Forgiven

Perhaps no story in the Gospel tells the story of redemption from a broken life better than the Parable of the Prodigal Son. In this story, one of the two sons of a wealthy man wandered off to a life opposite what God and his father wanted for him.

The story starts with the youngest son requesting his inheritance early. His father then divided up his wealth and gave the younger son his part. The son traveled to a distant land and, for a while, lived a life of luxury and sin. As we might guess, he eventually ran out of money, and unfortunately, his funds ran out at a time of great famine in this distant land.

Finding no other work than feeding the pigs on a farm, he took that job, frequently wondering why the pigs were fed better than himself. He'd hit rock bottom and was alone and destitute in a faraway place. He had no future and no support system; the friends he'd had when he had money were a distant memory.

With what little he had, he set off for his father's house, thinking that if nothing else he could get a job as a hired hand. Then at least he would be fed and sheltered and would have family close by. He prepared himself for his meeting with his father. He knew he would have to admit that he had sinned and squandered all he had been given. His thoughts were riveted on working hard to re-earn his father's trust. Over and over in his mind, he reviewed his past and was deeply regretful. He was finally at a place to admit his sinful past and ready to do whatever he could to regain a better life, even as his father's hired hand.

As he approached the farm, he was stunned by the reception from his father, who greeted him with open arms and accepted him back fully. A very different reception than he had expected. Out of joy, his father held a lavish party for all to attend to celebrate the return of his son.

His older brother was upset at the extravagant acceptance his father showed to the younger son, complaining, *"Listen! For all these years I have been working like a slave for you, and I have never disobeyed your command; yet you have never given me even a young goat so that I might celebrate with my friends. But when this son of yours came back, who has devoured your property with prostitutes, you killed the fatted calf for him!"* (Luke 15:29–30) All this was true.

His father replied, *"Son, you are always with me, and all that is mine is yours. But we had to celebrate and rejoice, because this brother of yours was dead and has come to life; he was lost and has been found."* (Luke 15:31–32)

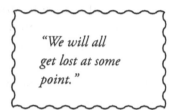

"We will all get lost at some point."

The son who had been lost was found. Like him, we will all get lost at some point. We will all want a second chance. We all will want to try again. Whether we are rich or poor, we will all fall. Falling is not the end of the story; it is about forgiveness and a heart that wants to change, the story of our faith helping us recover from our own brokenness.

✟ ✟ ✟

A Twenty-First Century Story of Another Prodigal Son

Mike Anderson went into a Burger King with a gun and robbed the fast-food restaurant. He was arrested, and at his court hearing he was sentenced to thirteen years in prison. The judge allowed him to be released on bail, and he was told he would be notified when to show up to serve his sentence. Mike went home and waited. Remorseful and regretful for leading a life of crime, he vowed, like the Prodigal Son, to fix his life; however, he first had to pay for his crime. Months went by and no notice came. Years went by and no notice came.

A clerical error had resulted in Mike never receiving a date to report to prison. He did not return to a life of crime and lived up to the promise he had made to himself and God. He returned to a life of faith. He started his own construction business. He volunteered at church and with youth football. He got married and had three children. He became well liked in his community.

Thirteen years later, the clerical error was discovered. Sadly, Mike was sent to prison to serve his time. His story received national and international coverage. Because Mike had led a faithful life over the previous thirteen years, people from his community and around the nation created a petition for his release and garnered thirty-five thousand names. Within a year, Mike was standing before a judge at a court hearing to discuss his sentence. Upon hearing Mike's story, in a matter of ten minutes the judge granted Mike credit for the time he should have been in prison—the time he had spent living up to his promise to God. With his wife and daughters, Mike walked out of court a free man.

In this famous story of the Prodigal Son, Jesus tells the story as an example of redemption, forgiveness, and a return to a life of faith. It is a story of a young man who squanders his wealth and lives an improper life; like Mike Anderson, he was on the wrong path. The Prodigal Son, like Mike, realizes he is lost. In seeking a change, the son returns to his father and confesses that he had gone down the wrong path. The father joyfully welcomes his son back, just as Mike's community rallied around him, which led to him walking away from his prison sentence a free man. Jesus uses the Parable of the Prodigal Son to show how God receives those who have changed through the gracious bounty of forgiveness. A forgiveness for all who have changed their hearts.

> *"Jesus uses the Parable of the Prodigal Son to show how God receives those who have changed through the gracious bounty of forgiveness."*

✝ ✝ ✝

"If you knew the gift of God, and who it is that is saying to you, 'Give me a drink,' you would have asked him, and he would have given you living water."

—JOHN 4:10

One of the most insightful stories in the Gospel about how Jesus helps broken people occurs in chapter 4 of the Gospel of John. It is the story of a slow but patient conversion by Jesus that lifts up the lowest of the low to become the first mass evangelist for Christ in the Bible.

Jesus is sitting alone at a well in Samaria—Jacob's well. It is noontime and a woman approaches the well. Jesus asks her for a drink. To us in the twenty-first century, this could be a story about a man in his thirties who is tired from walking long miles. He meets a woman with a bucket who can give him water. Seems simple enough, but it is not. It is a story with many twists and turns. It is a story of Jesus's approach to humankind. It is a story that resembles Jesus's internal conversation with us. A story that must be pulled apart. A story with a surprising ending.

The woman Jesus meets at the well is from Samaria and has had a very hard life. We know this from three clues that we are given at the beginning of the story. First, she is a Samaritan. The Samaritans were considered social outcasts by the dominant Jewish population. Second, she is a woman. In the first century, women had very few rights, and society was heavily tilted toward men. In fact, women were, in some corners, considered the property of their husbands. Finally, this woman is drawing water at noontime, the hottest part of the day in the Middle East. Most women would draw their family's water in the cool of the morning. It was also a community gathering time. This woman came alone, potentially because the other

YOUR FAITH HAS MADE YOU WELL

women of her community had rejected her. She lived a lonely and lowly life, an outcast for being a Samaritan and a woman, and then rejected also by her own people. Yet here she was, the lowest of society, unknowingly meeting with Jesus.

Jesus begins their dialogue with an innocent request: ***"Give me a drink."*** Stunned because a Jew is asking a Samaritan woman to do him a favor, she asks, *"How is it that you, a Jew, ask a drink of me, a woman of Samaria?"* Jesus ignores this question and proceeds to invite her into a conversation that is both revealing and designed to draw her deeper. He brings up ***"living water."*** His purpose is not to discuss the socioeconomic status in the Judean world. He has a mission for this woman. A mission that he could not spring on her immediately. He has a simple path of getting her to be accepting. A path that will lead to marvelous things. But Jesus is patient and knows to move slowly.

Imagine that you are this woman. We are used to people shutting us down because of our gender, social status, or past. It has been a hot climb to the well to get water for the day. Here sits a single man of the dominant culture asking for water. Would we think, *What does he really want?* Would we be suspicious? Would we be afraid? Would we bow our heads and humbly hand him water? Instead, this woman asks a simple question: *"How is it that you, a Jew, ask a drink of me, a woman of Samaria?"* A question of amazement. With this question, she reveals herself to be forthright and curious.

Jesus in turn tells her, ***"If you knew the gift of God, and who this is saying to you, 'Give me a drink,' you would have asked him, and he would have given you living water."*** (John 4:10)

She replies, *"Sir, you have no bucket, and the well is deep. Where do you get that living water? Are you greater than our ancestor Jacob, who gave us this well, and with his sons and his flock drank from it?"* (John 4:11–12) By saying this, the woman proves she is steeped in the history of the Bible and fully aware that Jacob was the great ancestor of the twelve tribes of Israel.

Jesus continues telling her about the *"living water"* by saying, *"Everyone who drinks this water will be thirsty again, but those who drink of the water that I will give them will never be thirsty. The water I will give them will become in them a spring of water gushing up to eternal life."* (John 4:13–14)

In this brief exchange, Jesus uses the woman's daily task of drawing water to tell her about a different way of living. A connection she will understand later. Jesus is not talking just about water but of faith in God. A way to change her life of being an outcast to being a faith-driven woman. A way to become accepted by God and her neighbor.

The woman asks for the water Jesus is offering but still does not know this is God talking to her through Jesus. Jesus tells her, *"Go, call your husband and come back."* (John 4:16)

She replies, "I have no husband."

Jesus knew this when he asked her the question to allow for a statement that would reveal himself to be more than a great prophet. Jesus says, *"You are right in saying 'I have no husband'; for you have had five husbands, and the one you have now is not your husband."* (John 4:17–18) Stunned that this random man would know all this about her past, the woman now knows that this conversation is about much more than just water. She replies to Jesus, *"I know that Messiah is coming (who is called Christ). When he comes, he will proclaim all things to us."* (John 4:25) Jesus replies to her, *"I am he, the one who is speaking to you."* (John 4:26) A clear statement from Jesus that he is the great *"I Am"* that visited Moses many centuries earlier.

The woman from the well leaves to tell her people that she might have found the Messiah, and she asks the leaders of her community to go back with her to see if this is true. Many from her community believe her because of the story she told and how

Jesus knew everything about her. They head back to the well and invite Jesus to spend a few days with them. After their time with Jesus, they proclaim to the woman, *"It is no longer because of what you said that we believe, for we have heard ourselves, and we know this is truly the Savior of the world."* (John 4:42)

Jesus had made the simple request *"Give me a drink,"* which led to the acceptance of his message by an entire community. Jesus did not condemn the woman because society had condemned her. Instead he looked past what her society thought of her, too who she was as a person. A curious person with a forthright attitude. A person trusting in God, who wanted to know him better. Jesus put aside the judg-

"Like many who have been broken, the woman at the well was healed because she believed and because Jesus saw greatness in her."

ment of her life and went straight at her value to humankind. She had been a broken woman, outcast by her people because of her past, gender, and an unforgiving society, but Jesus knew her differently. He knew that through her, an entire community would come to faith. Like many who have been broken, the woman at the well was healed because she believed and because Jesus saw greatness in her.

Brokenness is a place where many start their journey of faith. A point where we have led a life away from God. At our lowest point, we begin the long march upward to regain the inheritance promised to us all. Our own desire for a different life, combined with the forgiving grace of Jesus, heals us and moves us along on the journey of faith. We discover that Jesus does not care about our past but wants to guide our future. When we accept this future through our faith in the unseen, we are healed.

CHAPTER 7
PERSISTENT FAITH

"And will not God grant justice to his chosen ones who cry to him day and night? Will he delay long in helping them?"
—LUKE 18:7

Faith That Overcomes All Odds

Jesus has returned to his home in Capernaum. A great crowd gathered in and around the house. So many that even the front door was blocked. At the same time, four friends had heard about Jesus's arrival and picked up their paralyzed friend to take him to Jesus. They arrived too late to get into the house and found every entrance blocked. They knew in their hearts there had to be a way to bring their friend to Jesus. They persistently studied the house and began to debate the best method to get inside.

After some discussion, they decided to go to the roof of the house and create a hole, which would allow them to lower their friend inside. They climbed up and began to remove parts of the roof just above Jesus. When they had removed enough material to make a hole, they lowered their friend into the house. Immediately, Jesus saw the man and looked up to see the faces of his four friends expectantly looking back at him. Jesus saw in their faces a persistent faith of trust and hope. He immediately said to the paralyzed man, *"Son, your sins are forgiven."* (Mark 2:5)

Upon hearing this, the religious leaders in the crowd began to question the authority of Jesus in forgiving the man. Jesus responded by saying, *"Why do you raise such questions in your hearts? Which is easier, to say to the paralytic, 'Your sins are forgiven,' or to say, 'Stand up and take your mat and walk'?"* To demonstrate his divine authority, Jesus says to the paralyzed friend of the four, *"Stand up, take your mat and go to your home."* Immediately, the man stood up and went home. (Mark 2:8–12)

Four men knew in their faith-filled hearts that Jesus could help their friend. When blocked, they responded with a faithful ingenuity and found a way. A way that changed the course of a life. A simple act, driven by their hearts and full of compassion, was rewarded by Jesus, who saw in their faces a trusting and persistent faith.

There are times in our lives when we must lift up our neighbors when they cannot lift themselves. Maybe through providing a meal,

"A simple act, driven by their hearts and full of compassion, was rewarded by Jesus, who saw in their faces a trusting and persistent faith."

"Our faithful hearts sense when our neighbors are in need, and when we reach out, we can change the course of their lives."

or a ride, perhaps a prayer that is filled with a deep sense of compassion for our neighbor. Our faithful hearts sense when our neighbors are in need, and when we reach out, we can change the course of their lives. Our empathy for others and a persistent and trusting faith create a powerful healing.

These are times in our lives when we cross over the threshold of believing and know that the solution requires a persistent faith. A faith that relies on and trusts beyond what we physically see to what is unseen. They are times when we know that the next step requires an unusual persistence in our efforts. Obstacles may seem too high, but our faith drives us to carry on. We know our efforts may result in our momentary suffering. It is in this spot that we should not give up but persevere.

The apostle Paul describes this persistent faith and how it generates hope in Romans 5:3–5: *"We also boast in our sufferings, knowing that suffering produces endurance, and endurance produces character, and character produces hope, and hope does not disappoint us, because God's love has been poured into our hearts through the Holy Spirit that has been given to us."* In this statement, Paul describes the process of building a persistent faith. A faith that requires us to share with God the results we hope for—not to sit back and wait for our hopeful outcomes, but to work steadfastly with God. We then have the firmness of a faith that is sure that our honorable efforts, regardless of the hurdles we face, will be answered.

The four men were successful in getting their friend healed because they were sure their persistent efforts of compassion would be answered. They worked around the obstacles that stood in front of them and pressed on. Jesus, seeing this, healed their friend.

✟ ✟ ✟

Lessons from the Persistent Widow

In the Gospel of Luke, Jesus tells the story of a persistent widow. He starts the story by telling those around him, *"In a certain city there was a judge who neither feared God nor had respect for people. In that city there was a widow who kept coming to him and saying, 'Grant me justice against my opponent.'"* (Luke 18:2–3)

Widows in the first century had few rights or resources. Losing your husband and not having family to support you was a sentence of poverty and helplessness. There was no Social Security or other societal safety net. Widows were essentially helpless. To survive, they had to be persistent and tough. Jesus picks the widow, one of the lowest of society, to demonstrate that a persistent faith will prevail against even the toughest of circumstances.

The widow Jesus tells us about in Luke has been wronged by an unnamed opponent. In her town, the judge was corrupt and only cared about his position of power. He had little interest in God or his neighbors, but this was the only place of recourse for the widow: a corrupt judge who showed little interest in her or in doing right. Day after day, she showed up in his court to ask for justice. Day after day, this justice was denied. Finally, after many days of this, the judge said to himself, *"I will grant her justice, so that she may not wear me out by continually coming."* (Luke 18:5)

Jesus talks about this woman in the Parable of the Persistent Widow. He uses the figure of a widow to highlight the value of being persistent, even when we feel powerless. The judge in the story is the symbol of a society moving along, considering nothing but its daily route. Lost are people like the widows because they are not part of that route.

Jesus's point in telling this story is that our persistent faith in achieving an honorable outcome, even in the face of the evil, will produce results. He asks at the end of the story, *"And will not God grant justice to his chosen ones who cry to him day and night? Will he delay long in helping them? I tell you, he will quickly grant justice to them."* (Luke 18:7–8)

✝ ✝ ✝

A Persistent Faith Supported by the Full Armor of Our Faith

Patricia Williams worked selling time-shares for one of the largest time-share companies. Many of these companies use high-pressure sales tactics and often sell the time-shares at prices many multiples above their market value. Oftentimes, potential buyers are besieged by salesperson after salesperson, pressuring them to say yes. Patricia's company was no different, but she needed a job, and this was the best and only job she could find. She was new to this type of sales and was unaware going in of the harsh and hard sales tactics that commonly exists in the industry.

Shortly after being hired and trained, she noticed illegal sales practices and began to report them anonymously on the company hotline. Unfortunately, her input was not kept anonymous and she was fired.

"Finally, after four years of fighting, the jury hearing her case found in her favor. She was awarded $20 million in damages."

Angry at being dismissed illegally, Patricia filed a whistle-blower lawsuit claiming she was fired for the sole reason that she had reported these unlawful tactics. Patricia resisted accepting a small settlement from the company, and the company fought back. For four years Patricia struggled financially, resorting to eating out of her mother's pantry. The only work she could get paid little and, as the suit dragged on, her problems grew. Thankfully, her attorney hung with her and pressed forward. Finally, after four years of fighting, the jury hearing her case found in her favor. She was awarded $20 million in damages. The company was admonished; many former associates had testified in Patricia's defense.

When asked why she did not settle, Patricia replied, "It's been a long battle, but I had faith every minute that if I got in front of a jury of twelve unbiased people and an unbiased judge, they would see the truth." Her persistent faith in God sustained her against a more powerful foe. The apostle Paul describes this faith as being "fully armed." In Ephesians 6:11 he says, *Be strong in the Lord and in the strength of his power. Put on the whole armor of God.* Our foes will persist in their attacks and oftentimes seem insurmountable. Times can get tough. And at times we are left with only the armor of our faith.

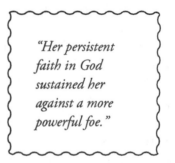

"Her persistent faith in God sustained her against a more powerful foe."

Many of us hit times of stress, perhaps not as severe as Patricia's, but challenging just the same. When we work in the marketplace, we are even more exposed. Temptation and schemes surround us daily. Having a powerful set of armor created by faith in God

Having a powerful set of armor created by faith in God surrounds us with protection."

surrounds us with protection. Very often in these battles there is a short-term loss, followed by a period of doubt. Holding firm in our faith when we know we are right becomes our rudder. A life well lived, one that includes faith, does not mean we will not be tested, but it does provide us with protection for these times.

✟   ✟   ✟

A Faith That "Bears in to God"

When I first met Kelly, I knew within a few minutes that she was a faithful believer. Through lengthier conversations, I discovered a curiosity and persistent yearning to know God. On the surface, Kelly is a happy person who laughs frequently. She is not a "party" person or a devotee of the ways of the world. She is one of those people you can count on for just the right answer and graciousness when it is needed. Below the surface, a deeper story of persistent faith exists. A faith tested many times by the fires of life.

Kelly's faith was developed in her youth by parents who committed themselves to living a faithful life. Kelly watched her parents persevere through difficult times as she was growing up. At the age of twelve, Kelly came home from school and discovered her mom crying in the laundry room. Her mother told Kelly she had breast cancer and would have to undergo surgery and chemotherapy. A painful situation for a mom with children to raise and the turmoil that would be created with this diagnosis.

Kelly's mom was treated and had surgery. Yet two years later her mother received more bad news: the cancer had returned. Another bout of treatment and recovery followed. Another period of time for her mother to worry about her own mortality and her children's lives without her.

After the second treatment, life was stable for a few years. As time wore on, the dulling and painful memories ebbed. Then came the receipt of more terrible news: the cancer had returned yet again. This time it had metastasized in her spine.

By this point in her life, Kelly had gone off to college and become engaged to her high school sweetheart. With her typical graciousness, Kelly's mother waited until the day after the wedding to have surgery and begin treatment again.

Kelly's husband, who had just started what would turn out to be a long and successful career, was transferred to an overseas assignment. Both she and her husband, despite being newly married, agreed that she should stay back and help her mother through her recovery. For eight long months Kelly watched her mother grow weaker as the cancer spread throughout her bones. For eight months Kelly lived without her husband and watched her mother weaken. For eight months she witnessed a gracious and uncomplaining woman live life to its end.

Kelly considers this period in her life a blessing. A time she could help her dad and mom. A period of observing two people deal with life's most difficult issue. Kelly says, *"That time was a precious, God-given blessing which helped me deal with her passing."* For eight months Kelly observed a faithful woman deal with her personal tragedy with grace, conviction, and courage. A final heroic lesson passed on from mother to daughter, so deep and intimate that it became a mirroring influence for the balance of Kelly's life.

Years later, Kelly's husband was promoted, which required her to move from her quiet life in the southeastern US to Los Angeles. She was nervous and excited about the possibilities ahead. She would spend four years in Los Angeles, and the amazing twists and turns of those years would test her belief in ways she wouldn't have thought possible. With the persistent faith she learned from her parents, she would have to bear in to God once again.

Prior to going to Los Angeles, Kelly had been drawn to seek a better understanding of the Holy Spirit. She was a life-long Methodist, and the Holy Spirit was not discussed much in the church she had attended. Kelly wondered and prayed about getting to know the Spirit. How does the Holy Spirit become revealed in our lives and our faith? Prior to going to Los Angeles, her primary question was how to strengthen her understanding of the Holy Spirit.

One thing we should understand is that Kelly maintains a constant dialogue with God in her life. Many times, while she is going about her day, she stops to talk with God. Asking questions and probing deep into the events of her life and how they are connected to God. Kelly's mind is always thirsting for answers about God and to know God more closely.

When she arrived in Los Angeles, her new community was not quite as different as she had expected. She lived in a gated community that somewhat resembled where she came from. She did the normal things, which included looking for the local supermarket and medical facilities for her family. She enrolled her children in school and prepared her house for her family.

At a school meeting with other parents, she saw another mother across the room and decided to meet and talk with her. They instantly connected and became close friends. Her new friend, Debbie, was also a faithful Christian. Along the way, another person named Dawn joined the group, forming a trio of Christian women who would together explore their faith, prayer, and lives for four years. Her friendship with these two women commenced a period of very deep exploration of her faith—deeper than any other time in her life.

Kelly was joyous to have two friends who were exploring their faith with her. It made Kelly happy and content. They studied scripture and the Holy Spirit, and they prayed together as their lives became intertwined. Their children played together. They dined together and shared life. They became the closest of friends.

On the day after Thanksgiving, Kelly and her family enjoyed a sunny day in Los Angeles. It was a perfect family day; they went to the La Brea Tar Pits to learn about dinosaurs, had lunch, and basked in the glow of a connected family. To Kelly, family is a joyous treasure. Contentment surrounded her in these moments. Together, they enjoyed a day that she called one of the most peaceful moments in her life. In retrospect, she felt that this sense of deep peace was preparing her for the news to come.

Later on this joyous day, she received a call from her sister-in-law that would bring her to her knees and create a guttural pain that would pierce her soul. Her dad had just been killed in an automobile accident. She was devastated and overwhelmed. Her second rock in life, her dad, was gone. Crying, she stood in her kitchen, and her five-year-old son walked in, asking why mommy was crying. Kelly gathered her strength and gently told her son that his grandfather had just died. Seeing his mother distraught, he went to the refrigerator and pulled down a picture of his grandfather and gave it to Kelly. *"Here is a picture of him, he is still with you."* Her son brought her comfort. It was the end of a day marked by extreme emotional highs and lows.

The following year, Debbie's young daughter started to have difficulty walking and riding her bike. Soon after,

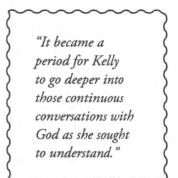

"It became a period for Kelly to go deeper into those continuous conversations with God as she sought to understand."

Debbie took her daughter to the doctor and received the worst news a parent can receive—her daughter had an inoperable brain stem tumor. Kelly and her friends began to pray for a cure. They maintained a belief that through prayer they could surround the child with the grace and Spirit of God. They earnestly felt that prayers could heal this innocent child. Despite their faithful belief in their efforts, Debbie's daughter died. It became a period for Kelly to go deeper into those continuous conversations with God as she sought to understand.

Near the end of the four-year journey, Dawn had surgery to remove her gall bladder. In the process, a mistake was made that caused her liver to fail. Over the next few months, every effort was made to reverse the effect of the mistake, including a liver transplant. Again, Kelly prayed, but Dawn never recovered, and died. Again, Kelly sought God to help her understand and the Holy Spirit to comfort her.

Three people very close to Kelly had passed in three years. Several years later she lost her sister-in-law unexpectedly—two weeks before Kelly's husband was scheduled for open-heart surgery. Later, Kelly's mother-in-law and a twenty-four-year-old nephew died in the same week. In all, Kelly had lost seven people she loved. She continued to find comfort in the Spirit and trust in the Lord through daily conversations with God. One evening while saying prayers with her son, he remarked, *"Heaven sure is getting full of a lot of good people we know."* A comment that Kelly will forever remember.

> *"She continued to find the comfort of the Spirit and trust in the Lord through daily conversations with God."*

Prior to my interview with Kelly, I knew her as an extraordinarily faithful person. You could see it in everything she said and did. Today, she is a Sunday school teacher and studies every aspect of God and knows her way around the Bible. She prays often and for everyone. She is persistent with her faith. Her heart rests with God.

Prior to my interviews, I always give people a Bible verse to read. Kelly's was the story of the mustard seed and moving mountains. I saw this faith in her and wanted to know where it came from. I had no prior knowledge of the four years in Los Angeles, the tragic deaths of her parents, or her other losses. Hearing these stories made me wonder why she had leaned into God when some move away from God during these times of stress. These seven tragedies heightened my interest to know why.

I found a clue through the verse about the mustard seed I had given her to read prior to being interviewed. She told me during the interview about a necklace that she had worn that contained a mustard seed—a gift from her father when she was a child. A precious gift from a parent as a constant reminder of her faith. A symbol from a parent who knew the value of faith and what to do when times got tough. Jesus says, *"For truly I tell you, if you have faith the size of a mustard seed, you will say to this mountain, 'move from here to there,' and it will move; nothing will be impossible for you."* (Matthew 17:20)

For Kelly, God continues to be her constant companion. It was God that she talked to during these many difficult periods of her life. Alone in the kitchen or driving in her car, Kelly talks to God. She truly does not know anywhere else to turn. This persistent faith, along with the guidance and comfort of the Holy Spirit, allowed her to endure the trials in her life.

✞ ✞ ✞

I Am Yours, God. Do Your Will.

My brother James, who is one year older than me, has a trusting faith so deep it permeates all that he does. As a salesperson for more than four decades, he learned by observing. He did not use the hard sell during his career; he observed where he could help. He would walk onto a job site and inspect all that he could before he talked with the purchaser.

James observed people and how they acted, and he learned over time the nuances of their behavior. He learned when they were frustrated and knew that on that day he would not be selling; he would be listening. He watched his customers and learned what they were good at. When a customer needed help or a reference, James would always have a recommendation of who to call. He knew when times were tough for some, and his observations helped him know how best to console them.

James also observes God. He watches the events of his day and connects those events to what he learned from his daily Bible lessons. He sits quietly in the back of the church and watches. He can tell who is struggling and who is happy. He uses these observations in later conversations with those people, to either encourage or help.

He is also a great citizen and football coach. He led the introduction of Habitat for Humanity in his hometown of Portland, Maine. He started the youth football program there, and over time it grew into a model for others to follow. He also coached the local high school football team, and as a result, the team progressed from not winning a single game before he started coaching to playing in the state championship numerous times.

On every trip around town with my brother, I saw how everyone knew him and loved him. There were always "hi" and "how are you" greetings from everyone he met. He is a quiet man who has a bounty of friends.

Each morning he reads the Bible and prays. On Tuesday mornings he goes to a men's Bible study. Mostly, during the day, he observes God at work. He developed his faith slowly in life. At first it was simply going to church; then his daily readings and his prayers. Most importantly he saw life through a lens that used the Bible and its teachings. He started noticing the differences between the ways of the world and the way of God. Over time, his persistence in these observations produced a trusting faith.

At the end of a long business trip to northern Maine, James was driving home on a cold and icy night. The road was treacherous and slick. Carefully he steered the car. He knew the process well from traveling these roads for many years in all kinds of weather conditions.

In front of him was a turn with a solid granite face at the end. As he entered the turn, his car hit the black ice that commonly occurs on these roads. Ice that is so thin, it appears to be the road and not a deadly hazard. No braking or steering could pull James's car out of the direct line to the granite cliff. With nothing left to do to save himself, he closed his eyes and trustingly prayed, "I am yours, God. Do your will."

James never hit the wall. Instead, when he opened his eyes, he found himself on the side of the road at a dead stop. He got out of the car to look at the damage. There was none—not a scratch. He had been positive he would hit the wall, but both he and the car were unscathed.

In the moment before the expected impact, James did not panic. He put his life in God's hands. A moment in his life built from observing and creating a trusting faith.

I admire people like James, Kelly, and Patricia. Their faith is trusting, built from a life of a persistent pursuit of God and a compelling yearning to search for the ways of God. Their faith is built on a lifetime of observing, questioning, and feeling God. A lifetime that forced them to "bear in to God" in difficult times. When they needed healing, they turned God's way.

CHAPTER 8

THE CERTAIN FAITH OF THE CENTURION

"Truly I tell you, in no one in Israel have I found such faith."
—MATTHEW 8:10

Where Else Can We Turn?

During my interview with Emmitt for this book, I became inspired by the certainty of his faith. A faith built on lifelong experiences with our Lord. Emmitt's faith is always present and unmovable. He grew up in the church and carries a commitment to the values of God. He has had a rich life that included being one of the few selected to go to West Point. His career was marked with success, from being a second lieutenant to becoming a two-star general. He served our country in Vietnam and during Desert Storm. When you meet him, it is obvious why he was successful; he is a man who is certain about things and a man you can trust.

In Matthew 8:5–13, we read about a similar military officer, a Roman centurion. A leading military figure who was part of the Roman army that occupied Judea in the first century. The centurion approaches Jesus and asks him to heal his servant. Interestingly, Jesus quickly agrees to help by saying, *"I will come and cure him."* (Matthew 8:7) Jesus knew something deeper about this man than what appeared on the surface. The centurion, even though he was a Roman official, also knew who Jesus was, and he knew he ranked lower than Jesus.

After hearing Jesus would go to his house to cure his servant, he tells Jesus, *"Lord, I am not worthy to have you come under my roof; but only speak the word, and my servant will be healed."* (Matthew 8:8) Two interesting statements are made here. First, the centurion calls Jesus "Lord." Amazing, considering his status as a high-ranking soldier in the Roman army who had pledged his allegiance to the Roman emperor. In the first century, the Roman emperor was considered a god and demanded to be treated as such. All Roman officials and soldiers were required to accept the emperor as the sovereign force in their lives. Instead, the centurion turned to Jesus, a potential threat and enemy of the Roman Empire, to heal his servant. What the centurion knew, despite his lifelong allegiance to the Roman Empire, was that Jesus was the "Lord," and it was Jesus he turned to for the healing of his servant, not the emperor or his Roman gods.

Secondly, the centurion knew that while Jesus was willing to go and help, it would create trouble for Jesus. For a Jew to visit the house of an important official of the occupying army would be considered a form of treason by the local population. As a Jew, Jesus would be violating the hidden laws of the Jewish people, but the centurion also knew Jesus's sovereign power and knew the healing could be completed without his physical presence. His statement of *"I am not worthy"* is also a statement that he knows the custom and wants no further trouble for Jesus.

Like any great general, the centurion knew what authority meant and how it worked. He knew Jesus was the *"Lord"* and that only Jesus could accomplish the task of healing his servant. Certainly, as a child and into adulthood, the centurion had known the Roman gods. He knew he served an empire that would frown on him turning to Jesus. He could have taken a more political and selfish route by staying within the Roman sphere, but he chose Jesus to heal his servant. His only goal in this moment was to help his servant.

Jesus knows all this and makes a bold statement: ***"Truly I tell you, in no one in Israel have I found such faith."*** (Matthew 8:10) Jesus knew the centurion was making an extraordinarily radical move in seeking him to help heal his servant. He knew the centurion was putting both his career and life at risk by acknowledging that Jesus was the *Lord* and by turning to him despite his cultural and political affiliation. Jesus knew that the centurion had a trusting and certain faith that was stronger than his allegiance to Rome. A faith stronger than even those who had been with Jesus these many months, watching him perform miracles, heal, and teach.

Emmitt's faith is like this as well. It is certain and formed with logic. Not everything had been a smooth ride for Emmitt. He lost his first wife to cancer far too early. He watched thirty-three of his classmates die in Vietnam. He survived Operation Desert Storm during the Gulf War in the Middle East. He watched others get promoted, not because they were better, but because of politics. Through it all, Emmitt hung on to his faith.

As all interviewers must do, I sought out answers as to why Emmitt had held on to his faith. The role of a writer is to give readers clear and honest answers to these questions. I asked, *"How did you keep your faith throughout the troubles of your life?"* He searched for a specific answer and could only say, *"Where else would I turn? Whom else should I trust?"* I did not accept his answer at first. I kept pressing, but Emmitt kept giving the same answer. His is a certain and trusting faith, like the centurion's.

> *"A certain and trusting faith is like a rock pounded by the seas, unmovable."*

A certain and trusting faith is like a rock pounded by the seas—unmovable. Those who have this type of faith know who the Lord is and know whom to salute. At the end of the story of the centurion, Jesus says to him, *"Go; let it be done for you according to your faith."* (Matthew 8:13) For people like the centurion and Emmitt, politics, worldly desires, and peer pressure do not affect their faith. They know who the Lord is and who to turn to for healing.

✟ ✟ ✟

Faith Inspired by Grace Filled and Inspiring Leaders

Dr. Kevin Miller was my mentor at Drew University as I worked on my doctoral thesis. During this time, Dr. Miller had a busy two semesters while he helped me and four others complete their work. He was preparing us for the difficult task of finishing the hardest part of getting a doctorate, our theses. He also taught classes, was the theological school's admission director, and served as a pastor of his own church. Dr. Miller was a busy person.

Mentoring us required reading our lengthy work and traveling thousands of miles to visit with us, from New Jersey to Texas to Arizona—all to help us formulate our thoughts and put together a coherent document that would pass the rigid standards required of a doctoral candidate.

Each email or call I received from him was filled with grace. They all started with "Grace and peace, Bruce" and ended with "Remain blessed in the Lord." Simple words that meant a lot.

Words of caring and a certain faith in our Lord. They were not said or written mechanically, but as a sincere gesture to remind us of our Lord and his concern for us. When I would see Dr. Miller in person, he looked me in the eye, caring about me and my progress. He did not give a superficial handshake, but one of welcoming. When he listened, he listened to learn. He probed to know more, and he was never judgmental.

Somewhat terrified that we would not complete this hardest of educational tasks, all of us talked with him here and there, by phone, email, or in person. Each of us knew Dr. Miller had the goods and that, if we followed him, we would be okay. He was not easy; he was hard. Invariably he would discover a spot where we were off track and suggest that we do better—not in a "command and control" fashion, but through an intellect that was inspiringly deep. Not one of us wanted to let him down.

Though he was very tough, he was also equally kind, never forgetting to tell us what he liked about our work and always knowing the context of the thousands of words we had written. Sometimes he would draw out things we should have written but had forgotten. Other times, through his analysis of our work, he showed us there was a different path we should explore. The presence of God was always with him, bringing to Dr. Miller's students a comforting knowledge that our work was sacred. He showed that to us and required us to remember it in return.

When he arrived to meet with my thesis advisory board, he had traveled over a thousand miles that day, and I was his last meeting. He said few words, but listened intently and asked very pointed questions. Never harsh or intimidating, his questions made us all think. His very presence raised us all. Then he was gone to travel many more miles.

We were all left in wonder: Who was this man, so sure of himself and so comfortable with listening and helping? His very presence lifted the standards of all in the room. He cared more about the task at hand than about his long day. He came to help but left us all aware of his presence of grace.

In John 20:21 Jesus said, *"Peace be with you. As the Father has sent me, so I send you."* Dr. Miller left us with this feeling. He came with the peace of our Lord and passed it on to each of us. Those of us who worked and spent time with him were all left with this sense of grace. There was never any doubt about the certainty of Dr. Miller's faith and of the grace he brought, not with flowery words or commands, but with his mere presence. His faith is certain and trusting in the Lord.

☩   ☩   ☩

Faith Makes Us Humble

Bob showed up at my door to fix a few tough things around the house. After many weeks of trying to make an appointment, he had finally been able to fit me into his very busy schedule. What I noticed quickly was his humility, and humility was his way of living. A quiet man of Mohawk heritage, he lived among us without fame but was sought after for the tough jobs.

He looked at my work, took pictures, and was remarkably thorough with his inspection. As our visit wore on and he got comfortable with my openness, he told me about his Native American heritage. He was one of the very few Native Americans who lived in a mostly white community, and he and his brothers served their nation faithfully, despite a history of broken promises by the country he loved. In fact, as a group, Native Americans serve in the armed forces at a higher percentage per capita than any other group of Americans. This heritage made it hard for him to understand why a gas pipeline had to be constructed through the land of a besieged group of people in South Dakota. But Bob was not judgmental; rather, he sought answers.

Bob worked most days for fourteen hours. As I said, he was highly sought after. His request for payment was always: *"Pay for my materials and whatever else you think I am worth."* The friend who referred him to me, Chris, explained that this was Bob's way. We always paid him more than what he had assumed we would, because Bob was good at his craft and humble in his requests. I am sure this unusual way of billing exposed him to being taken advantage of by a few. However, I am sure that his humility and the high quality of his work inspired most to overpay. Bob was humble, thorough, and busy.

"We always paid him more than what he had assumed we would, because Bob was good at his craft and humble in his requests."

Jesus makes an important life statement in Luke 14:11: ***"For all who exalt themselves will be humbled, and those who humble themselves will be exalted."*** He instructs us to be careful with how we view ourselves—to not overstate our successes and to be humble in acknowledging who we are. My friend Dick explains it by saying, "It's nice to be important but more important to be nice." Jesus also issues a warning that when we act as if we are better than others, we invite downfall. When we humble ourselves, we invite God's recognition of our humanity.

"When we humble ourselves, we invite God's recognition of our humanity."

Jesus describes this certain and humble faith by saying, ***"Whoever becomes humble like this child is the greatest in the kingdom of heaven."*** (Matthew 18:4) A childlike faith—one that believes without compensation, a faith that has become innocent and untarnished—is the attitude Jesus desires for us to achieve. Those who possess a humble and certain faith put aside their earthly desires and allow the ways of the world to dim. They move throughout their day focused on doing good and helping others. Bob had this certain and humble faith.

✝ ✝ ✝

Joyce, the Never Faltering Saint

Each year, a church that I attended in New Jersey, the Morrow United Methodist Church in Maplewood, conducts a two-week yard sale. It is the largest I have ever seen and certainly larger than most. Once a year for well over eight decades, the Morrow church is turned into a department store. The sole purpose is to raise money to help others. Every July, you can go to this church and find anything you want: radios, books, any type of clothing, china, toys, and even furniture. It is all there. Tens of thousands of dollars are raised every year to help those in need.

People from all over the community both give and shop. Each night of the sale it was exciting to see the many months of preparation pay off. Each night we all left exhausted after a hard day's work. In the preparatory phase, I was the truck driver who went out with two youths and picked up the furniture from homes where it was no longer needed. Every day, I was given a to-do list by Joyce Stibitz—the mastermind coordinator for this wonderful event. Joyce was constantly tugged from here to there, all of us wanting to know what was next.

And without fail, Joyce showed up every morning with a smile and a certainty in her direction. Never faltering, Joyce kept moving us forward.

Because of my size and background, during the sales period, Joyce periodically put me in charge of collecting the money from all the departments throughout the church. I would bring the money to the counting office and, in the quiet there, I would talk to Joyce. In these private moments, I discovered a richly faithful woman. Beyond being a powerful leader and coordinator, she held a faith that was not movable by those more famous or by the latest theories. Her faith was simply to love Jesus.

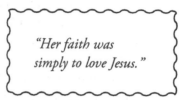

"Her faith was simply to love Jesus."

Joyce did not have great theories or thoughts about theology. She just did what she thought was right. Sure, she was not the best sayer of prayers or the most eloquent speaker. She just *did*. She knew the Bible and taught Sunday school.

"She was a force because she kept moving forward with a certain trust in the unseen."

She did wonderful things for her community. She was a force because she kept moving forward with a certain trust in the unseen. Joyce had a good life; her husband was extraordinarily supportive. She was a marvelous schoolteacher. She was extraordinary because she was wonderfully ordinary. She had no blemishes.

Her faith-life was certain and humble. She went to church faithfully every Sunday. She served on committees. She ran the largest yard sale in New Jersey, which was a year-round job. Everyone knew her, and she knew everyone. We all liked her.

She moved through life following the path provided by her faith. She was not a famous person because she did not see why that was important. On an evening where she knew I was exhausted from life, my studies, and the world, she told me, *"You have done enough; go home. I will pray for you and your life."* This was a moment that told me she cared more about me than her mission. In that moment when I was at my weakest, through a small gesture, her magnificent glory shone.

I always envy those with a certain faith. It makes them humble people. They are not looking for something bigger or better. They are certain their life is being led by God, and they know no other way to be. Like Emmitt, looking at me in amazement when I asked how he could be sure. Or Dr. Miller, who worked tirelessly to help aspiring theologians press forward. Or Bob, who worked hard for his customers and served his country with pride. They are certain in their faith and they are humble. They are like rocks on shore that, although pounded by waves, never move. Their faith protects them and heals them. They also help heal a world through their certainty.

CHAPTER 9

DO YOU WANT TO BE MADE WELL?

"When Jesus saw him lying there and knew that he had been there a long time, he said to him, 'Do you want to be made well?'"

—John 5:6

Reframing Our Lives to Become Healed

In Jerusalem, there was a pool called Bethesda where many of the ill, lame, and blind went to be healed. The pool was by the Sheep Gate, surrounded by five porticoes. Legend has it that the five porticoes represent the first five books of the Bible and are symbolic of the influence of Moses and his life. The Sheep Gate was the place where sheep were gathered for sacrifice in the great temple. In the early 1900s, after years of trying, the location of the pool was discovered, along with evidence east of the pool that suggested it was a place used for healing in the first century.

One man in particular had been going there for thirty-eight long years. Knowing this, Jesus approached him and asked the man, ***Do you want to be made well?*** The man did not answer the question; rather, he defensively complained to

Jesus, *"Sir, I have no one to put me into the pool when the water is stirred up; and while I am making my way, someone else steps down ahead of me."* (John 5:7)

Jesus ignores the complaint and says to the man, ***"Stand up, take your mat and walk,"*** commanding the man to give up his life of self-pity and to move forward. (John 5:8) Direct and to the point, Jesus reverses the man's point of view and heals him. Imagine trying the same method of healing for thirty-eight years and receiving no improvement. Perhaps the man was stubborn and insisted on only trying his way. Perhaps the man liked the self-imposed prison his mind had him trapped in. Perhaps for this paralyzed man, this was his only source of community. But before we judge, how many of us continue the same pattern and wonder why we see no differences in our lives?

Jesus heals him to break the vicious cycle so he can start a new life, no longer trapped by complacency. For years the man was stuck in a place of barely surviving, just hanging on to a desperate life, from which Jesus releases him.

Later the man is questioned by the religious leaders about who healed him. The man tells them he does not know. In response, Jesus later revisits the man and reveals who he is, but also says to him, ***"See, you have been made well! Do not sin anymore, so that nothing worse happens to you."*** (John 5:14) At this point the man knows it was Jesus who healed him. Jesus not only identified himself but gave him a plan for the balance of his life. A plan that tells him to avoid the debilitating impact of staying stuck in an unhealthy place. A place where he could forever become immersed. Jesus reframed the man's life plan so that it would no longer include being stuck in an unhealthy situation.

During my interviews for this book, I talked with a man named Clark. For most of his adult life, Clark had been a functioning alcoholic. Clark did not address the issue head-on for many years, and it simmered just below the surface, leaving him stuck and not able to fully enjoy the fruits of life. He had a loving family, a great job, and the admiration of his neighbors, but he was always just one step ahead of disaster. Clark reached the tipping point one fateful day when his life came crashing down.

> *Clark reached a tipping point one fateful day when his life came crashing in.*

In a stunned state, Clark still knew to move quickly from his car. He had just been involved in a horrific single car crash. He had gone off the road and hit a tree at a very high speed. The front end of the car was completely smashed almost to the passenger compartment, but thankfully no other cars were involved. As Clark surveyed the wreckage, he was surprised to be alive. He stood there, stunned and shaken, wondering how he only had a few bruises. In the deep recesses of his mind, it all came forward to him. He now knew he was worth something to God. He felt that God had intervened and revealed to him that he had plans for him—a different life to lead. He had to change.

Earlier in the week, Clark's wife had discovered he'd been secretly buying alcohol. Clark only drank alone, not around family or neighbors—just by himself. His family had a history of alcoholism, and Clark knew he had to avoid being seen this way. He knew his friends and family would confront him if he was discovered. So he kept it hidden. For a long while he had held this secret, but the discovery by his wife caused a mighty rift in his life.

A few days later, he was now standing on the side of the road thankful to be alive. He knew it was time to be made well. He stood by his car and was extraordinarily disappointed in himself and the secret life he was leading. He revealed to me that, more importantly, he was mad that he had also been lying to God. This thought seared and pierced his soul.

Clark is everyone's friend because Clark has an unusually high desire to help others. There is no task Clark can not or will not assist with. His employers loved him because he was always positive and trustworthy. He was the face of the company he worked for. Clark was also a faithful Christian and had the normal Christian life of church, prayer, and service to others.

Clark is always the first to lend a hand. A friend had an important sculpture that was broken. Upon learning this, Clark spent an entire evening fixing it. The next morning when the friend woke up, he went out and saw the sculpture fixed. This was how Clark treated his neighbors—silently and not looking for a "thank-you." He just fixed things.

As a child, Clark had grown up in a dysfunctional home. His dad would get very angry and abusive when he was drunk. Clark learned at an early age how to please his dad, despite his angry disposition. A carefully developed skill that protected him and his siblings. He learned how to defuse tough situations and smooth things over, skills that, later in life, would help immensely.

As Clark grew into adulthood, his dad's drinking grew worse. In one of the toughest moments of his life, Clark gathered up other family members and conducted an intervention. Clark knew the score and knew how to help his dad. With an amazing act of courage, he led the charge in forcing his father to see what he was.

Clark's father entered recovery and stayed sober for the remainder of his life. All from his son's courage and the moral compass that told Clark to do the right thing.

Now it was Clark's turn to deal with alcoholism. He now found himself on the side of the road in need of his own personal intervention. Although he was sad about disappointing his family, he was also remorseful at being dishonest with God. He had lived his life to be a good father and husband. He had lived his life to help others. Those who knew him knew he was the person to call at two in the morning for help. He was beloved by all, but he had lied to God, his family, and his friends, and things needed to change.

> *"While he was sad about disappointing his family, he was also remorseful at being dishonest with God."*

For many years Clark had avoided being healed. He put it off by saying to himself, *I've got this under control,* or *What's the harm?* He had helped so many, but he had not taken the time to heal himself. He kept putting it off until the bubble got so big it burst, leaving him on the side of the road, humiliated. It was time to finally get healed.

Clark went to Alcoholics Anonymous and began the long road back. Today, Clark knows he is an alcoholic and that it is in his DNA. Clark calls this disease the *"thorn in my side."* He likens this to the apostle Paul's thorn, which Jesus would not remove. Paul states in 2 Corinthians 12:7–9, *"Therefore, to keep me from being too elated, a thorn was given me in my flesh, a messenger of Satan to torment me, to keep me from being too elated. Three times I appealed to the Lord about this, that it would leave me, but he said to me, 'My grace is sufficient for you, for power is made perfect in weakness.' So, I will boast all the more gladly of my weaknesses, so that the power of Christ may dwell in me."* Alone on the side of the road, Clark now understood his thorn.

Clark has been sober for a while now and readily admits he is a recovering alcoholic. He's a powerfully wonderful man who helps others, but he put off for years the attempt to help himself be healed. Today, alcoholism serves as a reminder to him to stay true to God.

His family is intact. His job is going well. His neighbors love him. However, he still has his thorn, which he leaves as a reminder of the source of his bounty.

✝ ✝ ✝

Reframing Our Problems

In my coaching business, I often wonder, *Do they really want to move forward? Do they really want to get a new job, fix their business, or change their lives?* Many times, I see a lack of follow-through with the assigned goals from the previous week. I will hear, *"I had a bad week."* This is the point where I can either be judgmental or help reframe the individual's vision of how to move forward. Being judgmental fails to recognize that resolving the person's lethargy is part of the solution. Reframing our behavior expands the solution opportunities that are available to help us move forward and many times eliminates the lethargy in our lives that prevents us from being healed.

Many of us get stuck in a rut and cannot seem to make our way out. We skip over the fact that part of our problem is our habitual behavior. We keep failing and feel inadequate when we cannot seem to move forward. We judge ourselves harshly. We know we should do something different, but we cannot seem to rise up on a consistent basis to solve our problems. The solution is not to just promise to ourselves that we will be better. The solution many times is looking at the problem differently and being committed to a different habitual path. Instead of trying the same old way, try a different way.

✝ ✝ ✝

When You Move Beyond Your Fear, You Feel Free

When we pray and go to Jesus, perhaps he heals us miraculously. Or perhaps his life lessons heal us. Both can be true. Sometimes the solution is simply asking ourselves, *What would Jesus do?* It may seem trite to say this is all we have to do. It is perhaps too simple. Perhaps it is an overused platitude, but this question is still immensely valid in reframing our lives and circumstances.

Part of the value of the Gospels is that they lay out for us the lessons of life that Jesus wants us to follow. When we are stuck trying to solve a problem and our method of solving is not working, we must change the method. Many times, our solutions are not effective because we habitually use the same method over and over again. If we want to be healed, we must try new methods.

In the business book *Who Moved My Cheese?* there are four characters: two mice, Sniff and Scurry, and two humans, Hem and Haw. Each day, the four went to a cheese pile and ate. Over time the pile dwindled and eventually disappeared. Hem and Haw, while noticing the pile was dwindling, did little to find more cheese. Sniff and Scurry set out and found a new cheese station. As time moved on and the cheese pile continued to dwindle, Hem and Haw did not react to the change in the pile and became terrified. They resorted to anger, denial, and blaming to account for their situation. They debated and discussed their next moves but could not get themselves to move.

As hunger became a real issue, they eventually started looking for a new pile. The process was laborious and tedious. They endlessly debated

"What would you do if you weren't afraid?"

147

their various options. Eventually, Hem found the new pile that Sniff and Scurry had told them about, called Cheese Station N. As their mindset began to change, Hem and Haw thought of questions like, *"What would you do if you weren't afraid?"* and ideas such as, *"When you move beyond your fear, you feel free."* Slowly, over time, they began to reframe their perspective and to recognize the need to constantly look at things differently. They became well by reframing their lives.

✟   ✟   ✟

Changing Our Perspective to Become Healed

In Luke, after the resurrection, two women go to the tomb where Jesus was laid. To their dismay, Jesus was gone. *"The women were terrified and bowed their faces to the ground, but the men said to them, 'Why do you look for the living among the dead? He is not here but has risen.'"* (Luke 24:5–6) The women had arrived at the tomb of Jesus and found his body missing. Two angels suddenly appeared, and the women were terrified. They had been looking for a body and it was gone! All they had known was in disarray. Where had the body gone? The angels gave them a clue that Jesus was among the living and not the dead. He had risen. The angels reminded the women that Jesus had told them that on the third day he would arise. The women had heard this directly from Jesus before the cruci-fixion but at the time had not understood him. When he had spoken this message to them, what Jesus said did not fit with what they desired. It was too hard to comprehend, but now they saw it and remembered his words.

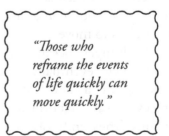

"Those who reframe the events of life quickly can move quickly."

Life is like this a lot. Change is inevitable. Those who reframe the events of life quickly can move quickly. Others of us, meanwhile, remain terrified of change. We stay rooted in the past and take on a cynical view of change. We hem and haw about why we must change.

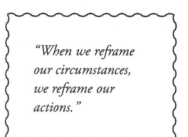

"When we reframe our circumstances, we reframe our actions."

We resist, but change is always inevitable. The more we resist, the greater is our fear.

The story of the risen Jesus changes this paradigm. It invites us to embrace change. As Haw said, *"When you move beyond your fear, you feel free."* This is true with both the resurrection and the smaller events of our lives. The resurrection is a reframing of our relationship with God. A God for the living and not the dead. A hopeful future with Jesus. In the smaller events of our lives, this is true as well. When we reframe our circumstances, we reframe our actions. Many times, it is the fear of changing that holds us back. Moving past this fear reframes our future.

✞ ✞ ✞

The Spirit of the Living God Changes Us

Daniel Ornellas, a worship leader for a church in South Africa, tells a story of the youngest of his three daughters, Frankie. On any road trip where Frankie was having a hard time, Daniel's wife would play "Spirit of the Living God" on her phone. The song would soothe Frankie. It changed her focus from what she was not getting to a spirit of contentment. Frankie would settle back and be filled. Over time it became a family worship song and lullaby. It drew the family closer.

The spirit of the living God changes us. It makes us investigate different places and through different lenses. We become able to see what we should see. For young Frankie, it was a soothing of the soul. For others, it will be a new direction.

In Luke 20:38 Jesus says, ***"Now he is God not of the dead, but of the living; for to him all of them are alive."*** This profound message from Jesus extends God's presence beyond just salvation. Jesus implores us to seek God out in our earthly lives, whether we are a family on a trip or a person looking for meaning in day-to-day life. Jesus asks us to be alive today. Those who live with the Spirit of God receive the benefit today. Like Frankie, we become soothed when we move from focusing on our earthly wants to focusing on a spiritual desire.

The world will try to steer our life canoe and create wants that are hard to achieve and misguided. When we are with the living Spirit of God, God helps us steer our own life canoe. Our life smooths out, and we no longer desire the things of this world. Instead we pursue the desires of God.

The Spirit of the God of the living creates a different point of view. A point of view that is not worldly, but spiritual. It helps us see that the latest fashion trend pales in comparison to the things of God. It reframes our lives.

When we let the Spirit of the living God in, it begins to seep into our vision. We begin to see things differently. It acts like a powerful vapor that, over time, creates differences in our perception. We begin to be kinder to strangers. We begin to hold doors, even when we do not have to. We begin to not become frustrated while standing in line.

"When we let the Spirit of the living God in, it begins to seep into our vision. We begin to see things differently."

We begin to know the meaning of Emmanuel: *"God is with us."* We stop doing the things of this world. We no longer make the trip to the pool of habitual behavior day after day. We reframe our perspective on life. We live our lives through the Spirit. We are soothed and healed.

CHAPTER 10

SEEING AND ACCEPTING THE SPIRITUAL WINDS OF FAITH

"Do not be astonished that I said to you, 'You must be born from above.' The wind blows where it chooses, and you hear the sound of it, but you do not know where it comes from or where it goes. So, it is with everyone who is born of the Spirit."
—JOHN 3:7–8

Being Born from Above

On this dark night near Jerusalem, Nicodemus is struggling to understand the message of God. As we have learned in previous chapters, Nicodemus was from the ruling class of first-century Judean society. He had nearly everything: wealth, a membership in the Sanhedrin, and social status. Yet here he was, trying to learn what Jesus had to offer. As stated earlier, Nicodemus felt compelled to find out more about Jesus, but he was trapped in a life of privilege. Like many of us he had a yearning for God, and deep in his soul he knew Jesus was the answer. Torn between the trappings of his life and the desire to know God, he visits Jesus. But Nicodemus is struggling, and he does not get what Jesus is saying. All that he had and knew was at risk, preventing his full comprehension of what Jesus had to say. Knowing this, Jesus was frank and to the point and says, ***"Do not be astonished that I said to you, 'You must be born from above.' The wind blows where it chooses, and you hear the sound of it, but you do not know where it comes from or where it goes. So, it is with everyone who is born of the Spirit."*** (John 3:7–8)

Jesus's point compares the Spirit of God to the wind. Jesus is simply telling Nicodemus that if he was with God or "born from above," then he would know that the wind—or life—is not for him to control. Those in commune with God or born from above understand the wind and the Spirit. Jesus is also telling Nicodemus that

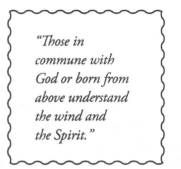

"Those in commune with God or born from above understand the wind and the Spirit."

he is trapped in the ways of the world. Matthew Henry, the famous seventeenth-century theologian, explains it this way: *"Thus the things of the Spirit of God are foolishness to the natural man. Many think, that which cannot be proved, they cannot believe."* Nicodemus is at this crossroad in his life. Does he accept Jesus's answer, which threatens his wealth, power, and status, or does he return to his life and still have a thirst for God that cannot be satisfied by the natural life?

Those of us peering into this story know the choice Nicodemus should make. It is a test in the school of life that has only one answer. Perhaps we feel like screaming out, *"Choose the wind!"* almost as if we are watching a horror movie and are encouraging the main character not to go into the dark room. We all know the answer and what we believe we would do.

This is the same question we are also asked every day and sometimes every hour. Do we choose the comfort of our life or the wind? Nicodemus has a lot to give up. Accepting Jesus posed a threat to all he had obtained in his life. To embrace the message of Jesus threatened all that Nicodemus had achieved through the world.

C. S. Lewis, the great English writer of the twentieth century, spent his late teens and early twenties angry at God. As he stated, *"I was angry with God for not existing."* An atheist for an extended period, he continually wrestled with God. He found church boring and religion a chore. His belief was that if God existed, he would not have designed a world *"so frail and faulty as we see."*

Lewis was a member of the Oxford University community, surrounded by people like W. B. Yeats and J. R. R. Tolkien. He was part of the intellectual elite of England during the early part of the twentieth century. Like Nicodemus, he could not buy into the winds of God. Like Nicodemus, his wrestling with God eventually ended because God became the only answer to a lifelong yearning.

"In the Trinity Term of 1929 I gave in, and admitted God was God, and knelt and prayed; perhaps that night, the most dejected and reluctant convert in all England."

He wrote his own conversion story, where he states: *"You must picture me alone in Magdalen [College, Oxford], night after night, feeling, whenever my mind lifted even for a second from my work, the steady, unrelenting approach of Him who I so earnestly desired not to meet. That which I greatly feared had at last come upon me. In the Trinity Term of 1929 I gave in, and admitted*

God was God, and knelt and prayed; perhaps that night, the most dejected and reluctant convert in all England." The searching had ended. Encouraged by his friends, like Tolkien, he was changed and reborn.

Both Nicodemus and C. S. Lewis went on to become wonderfully powerful Christians. Lewis wrote *Mere Christianity* and was instrumental in raising the English people's morale during the bombing of London in World War II. Many nights during the war, he spoke to the people of London on the radio to soothe their hearts while bombs rained down. Nicodemus eventually came out of the closet and acknowledged Jesus publicly. In fact, he was at the crucifixion and worked with Joseph of Arimathea to provide the burial tomb and spices for Jesus.

Life gets in the way of God, as it did with Lewis and Nicodemus, but God pursues us. We fall and do not accept the winds of God, but God's chase is never ending. Once we give in to our gift of grace, we are quickly whisked to life as another being. We are still *"frail and faulty,"* but our lives have changed.

The giving in to the compelling Spirit of God while satisfying our own yearning can and will place us at a crossroads. The path we take can make us well, both physically and spiritually, but it sometimes comes at a high earthly cost.

✞ ✞ ✞

Hearing the Wind and Turning Back to God

In the early 1930s, Germany was mired in fourteen years of hyperinflation, political turmoil, and poverty as a result of the sanctions imposed on the nation after World War I. What emerged was a Nazi regime, led by Adolf Hitler, that slowly gained control over society. Slowly, in order to not live a desperate life, the German people gave in to the terribly pointed moral compass of Hitler.

Dietrich Bonhoeffer, a young Lutheran theologian, stood up against this acceptance of the Nazis. He preached against Hitler in the great Lutheran church in Berlin, the centerpiece of the Lutheran worldwide church. He implored the people of Germany not to gain material safety by giving in to Hitler. He warned people from the most important pulpit of Lutheranism that nothing would be left standing in the end; even the very church that they were sitting in would be destroyed. In fact, the mighty cathedral of the Lutheran church where Bonhoeffer delivered his sermons was destroyed by Allied bombs during World War II.

Eventually, the Nazis seized control of the Lutheran Church and forced the Catholic Church to look away. In response, Bonhoeffer helped start a new church, called the Confessing Church. He organized a clandestine seminary to train young German pastors, but even this new church was compromised. Understanding the threat this church posed, the Nazi regime closed the seminary and continued to tighten its grip on every aspect of German spiritual life. Fearing for Bonhoeffer's safety, his friends encouraged him to go to New York City, where he would be safe. He went.

"Bonhoeffer knew he was not where God wanted him."

While in New York, however, he remained unsettled. Despite his wide acceptance and support by leading American theologians, Bonhoeffer could not shake the thought that he needed to turn back. Many advised him not to go. He would be safe in America, they said; in Germany he would be anything but.

Finally, in a desire to rid himself of the guilt he felt for not helping his German brothers and sisters, he answered the spiritual winds and returned to Germany in 1939. Bonhoeffer knew he was not where God wanted him. He left on the last boat out of New York to Germany prior to the start of World War II. Upon his return to his home country, he continued to speak out against Hitler. He was part of one of the many attempts to overthrow the Nazi regime.

He was arrested and thrown into prison, but he continued his ministry there with the other prisoners and the guards. In fact, many of the guards went to Bonhoeffer for spiritual help. Two weeks before the end of the war and the elimination of Nazi rule, he was executed. His executioner described his death as one of peace. A peace the executioner had not witnessed before. Bonhoeffer had turned back.

During the Last Supper, and before his fateful walk to the cross, Jesus said to Peter, *"But I have prayed for you that your own faith may not fail; and you, when once you have turned back, strengthen your brothers."* (Luke 22:32) Jesus knew that Peter would turn away. He was also sure

> *"Jesus knew that Peter would turn away. He was also sure Peter would turn back."*

Peter would turn back. He knew a crisis in Peter's faith would occur. Jesus knows that it will occur in each of us as well. Giving up our safety for a noble cause is a hard decision, but it is made easier when we follow the ways of Christ. We want to be safe but are left with a nagging feeling that we have let someone down. Our character fights with us. We are unsettled until we hear the spiritual winds and turn back to complete our task. When we do, we strengthen ourselves and others.

> "We all will have to turn back and confront our foe."

Most people do not have to confront the terror of Nazi Germany; however, we will all have something we need to turn back to. We all have something to do that is driven by the spiritual winds of our lives. This could be a troubled friend, a spiritual crisis, or perhaps a difficult business situation, but eventually, we will have to turn back and confront our foe. Jesus knew Peter would turn away and come back. Likewise, Bonhoeffer could not escape his mission. Similarly, we all have that thing that we need to turn back to. Maybe it is not as dramatic, but it nags us. Our peace will only come when we turn back. Accepting the wind and its course heals us and moves us closer to satisfying our yearnings to be with God.

✠ ✠ ✠

Faithful Integrity

Accepting the spiritual winds frees us in how we conduct our lives. Through this acceptance we change our perspective on what is important; we change our focus. We humbly put our neighbors before ourselves. Our moral integrity is heightened, and the combination of accepting God's spirit and putting our neighbors first, gives us a healthier and more sustainable life.

This is not to say that we should accept the spiritual winds for the sole benefit of benefitting ourselves. Quite the opposite; there are times when a by-product of this humble acceptance is our own sustainable success, but acceptance should not follow the thought of material gain; rather acceptance should always come first.

Often during interviews or in article requests, I am asked what the most important factor in a business's success is. Without hesitation I always answer, *"Faithful adherence to moral integrity."* Having integrity must follow gaining faith as its purpose. Integrity for the sole

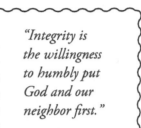

"Integrity is the willingness to humbly put God and our neighbor first."

purpose of being successful is not integrity. Integrity is the willingness to humbly put God and our neighbor first—in other words, living into the values of God and treating our neighbor as we treat ourselves. We cannot fully accept the winds if this condition is reversed. Our acceptance must be unconditional acceptance of the Spirit of God without seeking personal gain.

This acceptance leads to faithful integrity, which sometimes leads to personal success. For instance, I do not believe any business can be a sustainable business if it is not built on faithful integrity. Sure, there are businesses that will, for a period, be wildly successful despite not having integrity, but they will not stand up to the test of time. Similarly, no society can stand the test of time if its basis is tyranny and deceit. Eventually, it will be hit with a disaster that will cause it to fall. This has been a consistent lesson of history.

Conversely, having faithful integrity may cause a short-term loss of a sale, for example. However, the act of doing good will be rewarded through the test of time. As these various acts of goodwill mount, the business becomes more sustainable. Customers and employees learn to trust and admire the company's values, further enhancing their commitment to the company.

There will be those who take advantage of people who choose to have integrity. There may be loud and noisy incursions, but they are weeds and not the whole field. People who are driven by faithful integrity and spiritual winds will always be fulfilled.

Recognizing the spiritual wind is also recognition of the true power of life. It is identifying those motives in us that want to satisfy our earthly desires and making them secondary to God's. It is coming to a crossroads in our life and choosing the path of God through Jesus.

Accepting the spiritual winds is being born anew and becoming a new creation. We no longer worry about which way the wind is blowing or where it comes from. We begin to see the wind differently. We see the Spirit of God and have faith.

For Nicodemus it was a matter of being willing to risk his power, wealth, and status to accept God. After a period of wrestling with God, Nicodemus did accept and serve him. As did C. S. Lewis. For Bonhoeffer, it was giving up his personal safety to answer the call of God. In our own lives, where the drama may not be as high, it is pointing ourselves humbly to the values of God and helping our neighbor.

Once we accept the Spirit of God, we do not live by the Spirit of God to receive gain in this world. We live by the Spirit to combine the compelling Spirit of God, to be with and for us, with our deep yearning to be with God. We become healed spiritually, and we accept and see the course of the spiritual winds in our lives.

CHAPTER 11

WHEN MIRACLES DO NOT COME

"For surely I have plans for you, says the Lord, plans for your welfare and not for harm, to give you a future with hope."
—JEREMIAH 29:11

Struggling with Disaster

Many times, I have been asked to explain how God can exist when natural disasters occur, evil abounds, or after the loss of a loved one. I have always felt this is the hardest question to answer. While attending theological school for seven years, I discovered that there is no easy answer, and many other theologians have also struggled with this question.

Over time, I discovered that the resolution of the question *"why do bad things happen to good people?"* is far more complicated than a simple answer can provide. For some, these terrible events become roadblocks to accepting God. My personal answer, that these periods of disaster are transitional, does not always help. Personal grief resolution stands in the way. We will all have these moments in life, when God no longer seems real and quickly spoken platitudes will not work.

Many will try to make grief resolution the whole story of faith. It is not; it's only part of our faith-lives that is perhaps the most difficult hurdle. Certainly, it is a place where we feel most abandoned by God. It is also a place where those of us who help should be the most careful. It is a place that can be resolved.

In the Bible, the Book of Job explores the human emotions and thoughts that exist around these personal disasters. It is a wonderfully rich book that includes many of the emotions and advice that are valuable to those in grief. Relatable thoughts for those who are struggling. A place of personal identification for those grieving.

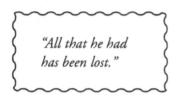

"All that he had has been lost."

Job has been hit with a series of disasters in his life. He has lost most of his family through a bizarre set of calamities. His wealth has been destroyed, and he sits alone covered with a horrible skin malady that stretches from the soles of his feet to the crown of his head. All that he had has been lost.

Completely in despair, he finds that the events that have destroyed his life will not leave his thoughts. As he turns these things over in his mind, they force him deeper into the abyss of hopelessness and abandonment. His wife blames all that has happened on God and implores Job to curse God. Three friends who have heard of Job's disastrous turn of events come to visit to soothe and console him.

His friends begin to give him advice. One suggests that perhaps he needs to repent for some forgotten sin he has committed. His friend implores him to search for that which he did wrong. Another friend questions his faith in God. Perhaps he did not have enough faith. One even suggests that perhaps

YOUR FAITH HAS MADE YOU WELL

Job deserves his punishment and should redirect his heart and resume a life more devoted to God.

All this advice does is force Job deeper into his mental pit of despair. As he sinks deeper, he says, *"I am a laughingstock to my friends; I, who called upon God and he answered me, a just and blameless man, I am a laughingstock."* (Job 12:4) His friends continue to try to explain that the reason for his calamities rests within himself, going so far as to say that no human is pure, and all deserve their lot in life. Through the myriad of explanations and Job's own thought process of trying to understand why, he remains at a point of dismal confusion. His thoughts move from searching for what he did wrong to questioning, why him? At times he defends himself to himself, feeling he has done nothing wrong. Other times he searches for what he could possibly have done to offend God.

Another friend, Elihu, arrives and rebukes Job's friends for their advice, cautioning them that though they may have felt they were helping, they were not. Elihu condemns their self-righteousness and rebukes Job for allowing himself to question his behavior and God's. Elihu implores Job to not forget about the majesty of God and to seek his counsel there.

> *"Elihu implores Job to not forget about the majesty of God and to seek his counsel there."*

Job is at a crossroads in his faith. Does he blame God or himself, or does he turn to God? After a long period of trying to determine what he should do, Job turns to God for his answer. God replies, *"Will you even put me in the wrong? Will you condemn me that you may be justified?"* (Job 40:8) God asks Job a question to help him see the nature of God. He asks,

"Where were you when I laid the foundation of the earth?" (Job 38:4) As Job continues his discussion with God, he moves deeper into his understanding of the nature of God. Finally, overwhelmed with the knowledge that God gives him through the questions, Job relents and is humbled.

The story of Job ends with him accepting the path of God. Job's health is restored, and his fortune is returned twofold. God blessed the later days of Job's life.

This story in the Bible has a happy ending, but more importantly, it contains the path to understanding and healing. Those in times of stress can identify with Job. We can relate to Job's inner thoughts when life is off course. We can relate to his disoriented state. We all know the crossroads that Job stood before, where we must choose between *"bearing in to God"* for understanding or blaming God and ourselves. For most, it is an identifiable spot of wrestling with life and God.

> *"We all know the crossroads that Job stood before, where we must choose between 'bearing in to God' for understanding or blaming God and ourselves."*

In the movie *Same Kind of Different as Me*, Denver Moore, the homeless man befriended by Deborah Hall, a true-life character in the movie, explains, *"There is no shortage of bad things that happen to good people."* There are times in our lives when things do not seem fair. Where we have

> *"There is no shortage of bad things that happen to good people."*

done our best, but bad things happen. In theology this is called "*theodicy*"—the study of why bad things happen to good people.

Countless books and papers have been written by many theologians to try to explain why. Countless sermons and prayers have been said. Some help a little and many miss the mark, but disasters are very personal and very complicated. For the individuals, it is a solitary walk with God. It is a personal confrontation at a crossroads. It is extraordinarily personal and intimate. There is no quick fix. Each one of these visits to the crossroads is different, similar to others perhaps, but not the same.

It is here where miracles no longer seem real, and life has dimmed. We enter a state of grief. The abyss of grief can be very deep and extraordinarily complex.

At a lunch meeting with an editor who was helping me with my books, he asked, *"How can you believe that God exists when an innocent child dies?"* The editor was recalling a difficult moment in his life, when his own child died. He was asking for my opinion as a Doctor of Ministry; surely, I would know. I answered, *"I am sure God exists from my own experiences in life, but I cannot explain to you adequately why this happened to you."* There was too much I did not know. I did not know the exact details of the moment when he had to stand at the crossroads, asking why. I did not know the formulation of his faith prior to this horrific event. And I knew to be extraordinarily cautious about giving a quick answer or to assert what I believed. I knew that God was real, but I also knew that I could never explain why something so terrible could happen. I could only be present and minister by listening. Grief is guided by self-determination.

Over time, the editor began to feel differently. Not through what I had said, but through a redirecting of his thinking toward God. As time wore on in our relationship, he began to see the value of God, saying at one point, *"I am starting to like Jesus."*

Another friend of mine, also knowing my background in theology, firmly asserted, *"I have divorced myself from God."* A few years earlier he had also lost a child and could not reconcile how this could have happened if God was good. Over the last few years, I have watched and listened to this friend struggle with his relationship with God. Sometimes he yearned to believe, but the pain of his loss prevented him from believing. Other times he was very indifferent to God. Today he continues to push forward, trying to understand, making gains, and then his grief causes him to fall back. Again, I have no prescription or pill. I can only listen and be present.

There is certainly *"no shortage of bad things that happen to good people."* Human answers will not completely help those in stress. We should be careful how we guide people who stand at this crossroads and understand that they will not get resolution from quick platitudes or simple answers. It is a very personal time in their relationship with God, and we should listen, be kind and caring, and be guides when we can. Grief is different for every person, and there is no universal formula.

What I do know is that we should not condemn or say, *"Your prayers didn't help because you lacked faith."* We should not look for failures on the person's part, as Job's friends did. We should be there in a *ministry of presence.*

The grief we feel at these crossroads of our lives is always unique and personal. My answer will never be complete. I can only share what I have seen others do or what I have done myself. Perhaps in one of these nuggets of insight is the key to which way to turn.

✛ ✛ ✛

"Blessed are those who mourn, for they will be comforted."
—MATTHEW 5:4

Loss is a part of life, and sadly, the older we get, the more we must endure. Whether through the death of a loved one, the end of a relationship, or the loss of a job, the process of grieving and recovering is difficult and very personal. Psychologists have identified that mourning individuals experience grief in five stages: denial, anger, bargaining, depression, and acceptance. A person must pass through each stage in his or her own time on the road to recovery.

These five stages should not be avoided. They will occur, and no amount of resistance will prevent them. Resistance will only bury feelings that will someday arise again. There is no prescribed time that each phase will last. There is no schedule of events. The only things that will help are listening and caring. This is a race that must be run with no prescribed time limit. Avoiding our grief only adds to the time we are in grief.

Jesus wants us to remember his promise that all who grieve will be comforted. Through both our physical and spiritual baptisms we become part of this blessing. He walks beside us in our grief, and through his promise he gives us reason to hope that we will recover.

In addition to death, many of us also feel a profound sense of loss when faced with disability or severe illness. An elderly woman in the early stages of Alzheimer's may grieve the loss of her fading memory, and her spouse may later mourn the loss of the woman he married, even when she's still physically present.

Loss can have far-reaching repercussions. Individuals facing illness, disability, or even the loss of a job may also suffer from intense anxiety and fear about whether they can continue to be able to provide for themselves and their families. Many who have lost a spouse may likewise struggle with how to provide for their families and parent their grieving children while they mourn themselves. No matter the type of loss, the experience is intensely painful, complicated, and difficult to navigate.

I have counseled many individuals who have lost a job, and as I guide them through their loss, I can see the process of grief at work. During the journey to recovery, individuals work through anxiety and fear as well as feelings of inadequacy and defeat. My assurances that there is a light at the end of the tunnel are no more than a temporary salve. Each person simply must work through the emotional process of mourning. It cannot be hurried or prescribed—it is a very personal process. During therapy, those in mourning will come upon roads they have to walk in order to continue their journeys. They will make discoveries and connections that are important and sometimes very surprising.

As we engage with those who have endured loss or are dealing with the process of grief, it is important to be empathetic. We should avoid offering platitudes, such as "it will be okay," or "just keep a stiff upper lip," or "have more faith," as these can feel dismissive and may not be true. Acknowledging and validating the feelings of those in mourning and allowing them to share their thoughts

> "The journey through grief can be incredibly difficult, and for those who are in grief, time grinds on slowly."

and express their emotions is the best way to help. They are traveling difficult and unfamiliar roads, and their emotions will fluctuate, often throughout each day and week. As they proceed through the five stages, we can become their biggest allies simply by loving them and listening to them. The journey through grief can be incredibly difficult, and for those who are in grief, time grinds on slowly.

In Matthew 5:4, Jesus says that mourners will be comforted. The word "will" gives us hope for the future. Through our baptism, we belong to a faith that gives us the assurance that the valleys of life are temporary. While our losses will never be fully recovered, we never lose the love of God. The gift of God's love does not just occur because of our physical baptism; it occurs through our spiritual acceptance of God's promises. The promise in Matthew 5:4 encourages us to keep our faith, even during the darkest moments in our lives. Jesus promises us we will be comforted.

✢ ✢ ✢

The Tides of Life

Our greatest enemy in these periods of stress is time. We want things to be righted quickly. We want to have our answers quickly, and we want to be free of the bonds of sadness. These periods of time can stretch on endlessly, and the mountaintop of relief can seem too far away.

Charles Allen, the great pastor, writer, and radio host of the mid-twentieth century, describes this period as the tide going out. He says, *"Sometimes all we can do is wait for the tide to come back in again."* This is easy to say for those of us not in stress, but for the person grieving, the wait can seem endless. It is here we must reconcile with the sovereign nature of God.

After spending two weeks on an island along the coast of Georgia, Charles Allen created a reflection on the tides. In this reflection he quotes Psalm 95:5, *"The sea is His, for He made it."* Adding to this, Allen says, *"Such assurances give one a deep sense of security. With a God like our God, we know that we really have nothing to fear."* Sitting and watching the sea reinforced Allen's faith. In essence, it was a two-week statement by God to him on the majesty of the sea and of God himself.

Others have experienced similar feelings. When I asked my friend John Robinson—a well-regarded friend by many of his neighbors with a knack for speaking common sense with immense clarity—about his faith, he replied, *"How else could the deer glide so effortlessly into the trees, where no one of us could go? Or watch the birds fly to and fro; we only have to watch the things of nature to know that only God could create this elegance."*

As a pastor, Charles Allen had seen and helped many distressed people. He noticed the similarity between their grief and the tides he watched for two weeks. The tide will come in and then go out. As with our lives, there are highs and lows, but the tide will always come back in. Believing this is the core of faith. Regardless of our present circumstances, God will always be with us and is sovereign. To have this belief requires an observation outside our lives. Perhaps it is an observation of the rhythmic tides. Perhaps the beauty and elegance of nature. Perhaps it is seeing great acts of mercy. Perhaps it is knowing that the night is always the darkest and coldest before dawn. The reconciling of our grief with the sovereign nature of God tells us which path to take.

> *"As with our lives, there are highs and lows, but the tide will always come back in. Believing this is the core of faith."*

☩   ☩   ☩

"We know that all things work together for good for those who love God, who are called according to God's purpose."
—*ROMANS 8:28*

Like Charles Allen, my dad and I sat on a bench overlooking the never-ending crashing of waves at Pemaquid Point, an inspiring place on the coast of Maine. We talked about life as my wife and my mom shopped at the gift store and explored the surrounding areas of the park. My dad can no longer walk long distances and sometimes gets confused. On this bench, I heard stories about his past and enjoyed the companionship of a man who was the earthly rock of my life. At times, I could hear that guiding voice I remember hearing as a teenager. At times, I could see the man who provided for his family and kept us safe. At times, I could see the man who generously provided the funds for my education and only asked me to do my best. Other times, I could see the lights of his brain flickering, a signal it was beginning the long process of shutting down.

As I sat there, I wondered why I was not in stress watching the inevitable occur. Why was I not despondent or near tears? Why did I not get frustrated earlier in the day, when it took him fifteen minutes to find his coat, so we could leave? Why was I okay to wait for him while he took deliberate steps to walk a short distance? Partly out of respect for this great man who had lived his life the right way. Partly knowing that I owed it to him for the times he waited patiently for me to get his lessons on life. In addition, it was because I knew he was going to be safe. I knew that Jesus was surrounding him and patiently helping him with the inevitable. I knew that through his baptism and the way he had lived his life, he was getting ready to go home.

God does not always give us what we want. Many times, tragedies occur that seem senseless, making us ask why God would let these things happen. I am not sure of the answer, but I do know God does not want or approve of evil. But evil, disease, and aging exist. They are not something we can avoid; they are inevitable. In the Book of Romans, the apostle Paul

DR. BRUCE L. HARTMAN

tells us that all things work together for good. Believing this is hard at times, especially when we cannot fully comprehend the reasons. This is the moment of faith. Our personal test of which way we turn. Although it would be easy, but trite, to try to explain in human terms the cause of evil, tragedies, disease, and aging, it is important that we become pastoral and remember that *"all things work for God's purpose."* It is at these moments that we turn toward one another and God.

I can hope for my dad. I can wish that he would not get older, but I do not control that outcome; certainly, if I did, I would make it happen. Time moves on, and he sits on his couch at home and nods off to sleep. He will forget why he said something. His recollections of the past can be very disjointed. He will irritate my mom and make her worry, but he still sits with the grace that he uses to live life.

On our way home, stopped at a red light, I drifted off, daydreaming about an unimportant thought. The light turned green, but I did not notice, lost as I was in my daydreaming. I was brought back with the words *"Bruce! The light is green."* Instantly I snapped back to the present and stepped on the gas, comforted by hearing the familiar voice from my youth —my dad's.

✝ ✝ ✝

A Life Redeemed

Denver Moore, one of the main characters in the movie *Same Kind of Different as Me*, was born into poverty. During his childhood he had little, and what he had was hard-won. Nothing came to Denver easily. The embers of goodness that reside in children never had a chance to flicker in him. It was replaced by a life of scarcity that required a fight for all he received, a constant pushing for sustenance, enhanced by his own physical strength. He never attended school. As a young adult he was homeless. In his youth, he was roped and dragged by the Ku Klux Klan for helping a white woman change a flat tire.

He found a rusted gun, with no cylinder, and tried to rob a bus. He left the bus after being unable to get the change out of the coin box He was arrested and sentenced to twenty years in the notorious Angola Prison. Any ember of goodness in him dimmed even more. Knowing no other way, Denver had taken the wrong path at every crossroads of his life. A life where he never saw the majesty of God.

After twenty years, he was released and put back on the streets. He slept on grates by a hotel or near a soup kitchen. He carried a large bat to protect himself and claim his space.

Deborah Hall was struggling with her own life. The affluent wife of a successful art dealer, she was beset by anguish that she should be doing more and not just consuming life. Her husband was growing distant and unavailable. In a restless sleep, she had a dream about a powerfully built man who could help her recover her purpose.

In her frustration, she started helping at a center that served homeless people by raising money and serving food. Through a crisis in her marriage she was able to convince her husband, Ron, to also help. Reluctant at first, he soon stood beside her serving food.

A man would regularly come in and insist on not just one meal, but two. Any attempt to dissuade the man was met with anger, and the staff always relented to ensure calm. One day there was not calm, and the man used his bat to threaten people and damaged a significant artifact of the shelter.

During this event, Deborah recognized the man as the one from her dream. She asked her husband to go talk with him. Reluctantly, Ron followed the man out of the shelter. The man went behind a building and Ron went after him. There Ron

> *"Ron saw the ember of goodness in the homeless man flicker in an act of unselfishness."*

saw a great act of charity; the large, angry man gave one of his two meals to a homeless person confined to a wheelchair. Ron saw the ember of goodness in the homeless man flicker in an act of unselfishness. He had not been selfishly asking for two meals for himself but wanted one for his friend. The man was Denver Moore. From that point, Ron slowly began to engage the man to build up trust. A trust that would develop into a wonderful fourteen-year revival of both their spirits. Denver Moore became a member of the Hall family and was at Ron's side at the country club, social events, and family gatherings. After a lifetime of denials, Denver was receiving.

Deborah died of cancer a few years later, but not before developing the center into a model of how to help. Denver was there to console his friend Ron and delivered the eulogy at Deborah's funeral. With Ron, he wrote the book that became the movie *Same Kind of Different as Me.*

> *"Despite all that had happened to him, that small ember of goodness that for many years had been dormant roared into a flame."*

Denver died in 2012. He left a wonderful legacy of giving in those fourteen years. He helped raise over $70 million for the homeless. He helped his friend recover from the loss of his wife. His last years were about giving and not taking. His last years were spent taking a different path at the crossroads of life. His last years included the tide of his life coming in. Despite all that had happened to him, that small ember of goodness that for many years had been dormant roared into a flame.

Miracles do not always happen the way we want, leaving us frustrated and in a prolonged period of grief. For some, like Denver Moore, life starts out bad, and we do not get the chance to excel and experience a life of bounty. For the parent who loses a child, no pain can be greater. We ask, *"Why, God, did this have to happen?"* For some it is losing a job despite their good work or being denied a promotion even though they were the most qualified. When miracles do not happen, life is at its toughest.

When we find ourselves at the inevitable crossroads, do we blame God, or do we bear in to God? The answer to this question is extraordinarily personal. Denver took the wrong path too many times because it was all he knew. Some must learn a hard lesson first. For others it is unexplainable. The story

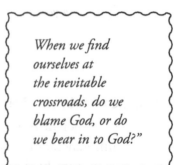

When we find ourselves at the inevitable crossroads, do we blame God, or do we bear in to God?"

of Job is in the Bible to help guide us. In this story we see all the human thoughts and advice, but the path to the answer is through our sovereign God, no matter how angry we are. Who else made the stars in the sky or allows the deer to glide elegantly in the woods? Our healing through faith lies within the decisions we make at the inevitable crossroads of life.

EPILOGUE

"Rise up, walk through the length and breadth of the land,
for I will give it to you."

—GENESIS 13:17

Walking the Length and Breadth of Our Faith

The great father of our religious heritage, Abraham, was from the tenth generation since Noah. His father, Terah, had taken Abraham from his home in Ur to journey through the land of the Canaanites, but the father never made it into Canaan. He stopped instead in Haran, and there Terah died.

After his father's death, Abraham was spoken to by God, who said, *"Go from your country and your kindred and your father's house to the land that I will show you."* (Genesis 12:1) Abraham initially obeyed and began a long journey throughout the region, taking with him his immediate family and nephew, Lot. Along the way they were beset by many struggles, including a famine. Desperate to avoid the loss of his health and wealth, Abraham led them into Egypt, a detour from the request of God to go to the land he would reveal to Abraham. Abraham, like his father, became distracted and, lacking in faith, moved away from God's plan.

While in Egypt, he implored his wife, Sarah, to tell Pharaoh and the Egyptians that she was Abraham's sister, not his wife. This was an act of concealment to avoid Abraham being murdered by potential suitors of Sarah. For Sarah was beautiful, and Abraham was sure that Pharaoh would murder him to possess her.

The plan worked for a while. Sarah was fully accepted in Pharaoh's house, and Abraham was treated well by the Egyptians. Pharaoh took Sarah as his wife, but he soon developed sores and other plagues caused by God. Pharaoh, knowing these events were caused by God, confronts Abraham and asks him why he lied. Why did he not tell Pharaoh that Sarah was his wife? Fearing more retribution from God, he banished them all from Egypt.

Along the way, the herds of both Abraham and Lot grew, causing great animosity between them. Abraham tells Lot to choose a place where he would go, and Abraham would take whatever place was left. Lot chose a large parcel of land that would be best for his herds, but which also contained the city of Sodom—a place that was notorious for its wickedness and sinful behavior.

Lot moved his herds and settled in the city of Sodom. Abraham took over what was left. With a final settlement, after years of traveling to Canaan and being distracted by his own fears and hearing the siren calls of other lands, Abraham was in the land where God wanted him to be.

God then issued a request to Abraham to *"rise up, walk through the length and breadth of the land, for I will give it to you."* (Genesis 13:17) Now that Abraham was finally where he should be, God told him to inspect all that he owned—to walk its length and breadth, to immerse himself in all that God was giving him, and not to just see the trees and water, but to be with the land. To explore every facet of this land that he had inherited from God.

Metaphorically, we can see this same thing in our lives. Our faith is what God wants us to explore and become completely immersed in. Not just to stand by and watch the unfurling of our faith, but to experience and invest our energy in our faith. To move beyond just saying our prayers and reading the Bible, to fully exploring our prayers and the Bible. To become deeply immersed. To learn the ways of the world and what to avoid. To wonder at the majesty of all creation. To wonder about the stars, to observe the spiritual winds of our lives. To not become attached to the shiny and temporary glimmers of the ways of the world, but to our faith.

> *"Our faith is what God wants us to explore and become completely immersed in."*

✟ ✟ ✟

Walking the Trails of Our Faith

On a recent hike of the Appalachian Trail in Massachusetts, a friend of mine exclaimed, *"This is boring! Aren't there any vistas to see?"* We were on a stretch of this famous route, which stretches from Springer Mountain in Georgia to Mount Katahdin in Maine, encompassing well over two thousand miles. This stretch we were walking on had no waterfalls or great vistas or flowing streams. It was a seven-mile stretch that flowed over small rises and descended into expansive valleys. Nothing existed on this silent pathway except ferns, large green trees, rocks to avoid, and a brown path. That's all there was. It was a place to wander and wonder on the way to the next segment.

It took me back to my professional career and reminded me of the many days and months where all I had to do was my job. Ambition always pushed me to want to take the next great step in my life. Just doing my job was not enough. What was next for me would ramble in my mind, luring me to put my focus on the excitement of a new position and the challenges ahead. However, most of my days were spent walking through these stretches of my career, just doing my job, being a faithful employee, and helping my company.

When we are young, we are told of the great things that lie at the end of the segment of the trail we are on. We look expectedly to that future. Along the way, we hope that our efforts lead to an extraordinary life, but during our walk through life, we will meet many ordinary people and walk by many ordinary places. Through these seemingly ordinary people and places we find extraordinary stories. We only need to stop and observe to find them. They frame our lives, values, and friendships. It is in these moments that we find the most extraordinary things— and our faith.

The verse in Genesis at the opening of the Prologue is about God's promise to Abraham. God was about to give him a land that would be the source of our great faith, but first, Abraham had to walk its entire breadth to see the ordinary and learn about its ways. A walk where observing was more important than the finish. Surely, Abraham would see great vistas, running streams, and waterfalls, but most of his journey would be with the ordinary. Jesus himself wandered thousands of miles in his great mission to reveal God's values to humanity. We read about his miracles and those he helped, but most of his time was spent just "walking the trails."

> *"God's promise is an extraordinary life, when we have walked the length and breadth of his land."*

Surely, when we walk with faith and an eye toward the values of Jesus, we will see great things, but most of our walk will be in everyday life. Our careers might have those days of great success, but most days will be spent doing ordinary things. Life will be just doing our jobs, raising our children, and living a life. God's promise is an extraordinary life, when we have walked the length and breadth of his land. A life extraordinary not just in what we see in the end, but in what we experience along the way.

✞ ✞ ✞

"Very truly, I tell you, the Son can do nothing on his own, but only what he sees the Father doing; for whatever the Father does, the Son does likewise."
—*John 5:19–20*

Like Abraham and many of our ancient predecessors, we are challenged many times in our faith. At these crossroads we are confronted with which path we ought to take. In the world of ethics, the critical word is "ought." Essentially, when we are confronted with a difficult situation, our mind asks us, *What ought I do?* It can be a simple question, like *Should I hold the door for the other person? Should I stop and help a person in distress even though I have a lot of errands to run?* Or on a different scale, we are confronted with, *Should I tell my boss or the CEO that what my company is doing is wrong? I see a manufacturing defect that no one will notice; should I tell someone?* Each day we are confronted with these questions. Each day we must make these personal decisions. Each day our lives are a class on ethics. *What ought we do?*

Beyond the ethics of doing the right thing, we must also show faith by having the courage to do the right thing. If we truly believe and have faith in the unseen, then we will not hesitate to do those "right"

> *"Being bold in our faith leads us to do what God would have us do."*

things, even if doing so might put us at some personal risk. Being bold in our faith leads us to do what God would have us do. A faith that if we choose a path for the right reasons, God will give us *"a future with hope."*

When we bring Jesus into our thought process, ethics turn into Christian ethics. We then begin to ask, *"What would Jesus do?"* Sounds simple, but it is not. Competing with what Jesus would do is our natural selves. Like Abraham, we have our own desires and needs. We need to pay our bills. We need to earn a living in order to do that. We want our worldly needs satisfied. Sometimes these needs will conflict with what Jesus would have us do.

I know a woman named Beth, who was homeless and fighting hard to regain her footing so she could raise her child in a home like she saw other mothers do. She worked at a local Dunkin' Donuts in a job that sometimes had her scraping gum off the bottom of the tables. Her boss was abusive and ranted at her throughout her shift. Each day, she went back to her shelter with a little more money to get her freedom. On the Christmas Eve of her one-year journey of homelessness, she left work and found a woman in the parking lot who was in need. It was a dark, rainy night, and the woman had not recently eaten and was rummaging in the trash bin behind the store. With what she had earned in tips that day, Beth took the woman into Dunkin' Donuts and bought her a meal. She sat with the woman and listened to her story. On that rainy Christmas Eve, she drove back to her shelter wondering if she had done enough for the woman.

Beth eventually got an apartment and left her job to work at a better place. The next fall she was able to put her child on a school bus for her first day of school. She was able to go to a job where she was respected. She continued to wonder if she had done enough on that Christmas Eve.

Deciding what we ought to do seems complicated, but Jesus gives us a simple blueprint when he says, **"but only what he sees the Father doing; for whatever the Father does, the Son does likewise."** Regardless of our natural circumstances, Jesus tells us to act in a manner that we envision how God would act. He asks us to act without fear of loss, but through our hearts. We should not overly ponder the event, but let our knowledge of God through our heart tell us what we "ought" to do. We should walk on our path of faith to explore the length and breadth of our inheritance. An inheritance that will heal and free us.

"We should walk on our path of faith, to explore the length and breadth of our inheritance. An inheritance that will heal and free us."

This walking the length and breadth of our faith-land is our personal investment—an action that ensures an inheritance and our own spiritual healing. The woman who was bleeding for twelve years followed this course by seeking out Jesus. Her very struggle to force her way through crowds that rejected her was an act to claim her inheritance—to later hear from Jesus, *"Daughter arise, your faith has made you well."*

Or like our first visit with Cindy in the Preface, who reached out to her friends when Scott was in trouble. A plea of certainty that through her community's prayers and her own faith, Scott would be made well.

Likewise, Clark, a powerfully gentle man with a helping heart, delayed his arrival to his promised land by hanging on to the debilitating disease of alcoholism, only to finally find himself on the side of the road having narrowly escaped death. At this point, Clark finally decided to no longer conceal but to embrace a new life of faith without alcohol.

Many of the great characters of our faith also took this long path to their own inheritance. Peter, whom Jesus called the "rock," many times denied his faith. Augustine led a life very far away from God in constant pursuit of the truth, never able to quench his yearning. Later, in a garden of Milan, he finally succumbed and went on the way to a life of faith.

Our faith-lives are journeys that will lead to healing, both spiritually and physically. There will be many times in our life journey when we will stand at a crossroads, deciding what path to take to claim our healing and inheritance. It is a journey made easier through prayer, the Bible, and our faith. A journey where we are joined with Jesus. Our journey will require a personal investment in our faith development. We will always be asked, *"Take up your mat and walk."*

On this continuing path of our lives, Jesus will tell us, *"Your faith has made you well."*

ABOUT THE AUTHOR

Dr. Bruce L. Hartman is an author and Christian advisor committed to "walking with people into a brighter future" as they navigate life.

Bruce's first book, *Jesus & Co.*, has received rave reviews and is rated a five-star book on Amazon. The book intersects the world of the twenty-first worker with the first century teachings of Jesus. The book received the Readers' Choice Award in the fall of 2018. Prior to entering the world of ministry, he was a Fortune 500 CFO where his skill with working with people created many changed lives.

Leaving the corporate world, he graduated in 2013 with a Master of Divinity from Drew University Theological School, earning the Daniel P. Kidder Award for excellence in Pastoral Care. In May of 2018, Bruce received a Doctorate degree from Drew.

Hartman's passion for mentoring people throughout his career has enabled him to repeatedly develop talent into C-Suite executives, encourage employee engagement and development at all levels, and transform organizations into high-performing centers of excellence.

He presently serves as President and on the Board of Directors of A Future with Hope, as well as serving on the boards of Drew University and United Methodist Development Foundation.

Find the author at www.brucelhartman.com